TRUTH TELLING

ALSO BY MICHELLE GOOD

Five Little Indians

TRUTH TELLING

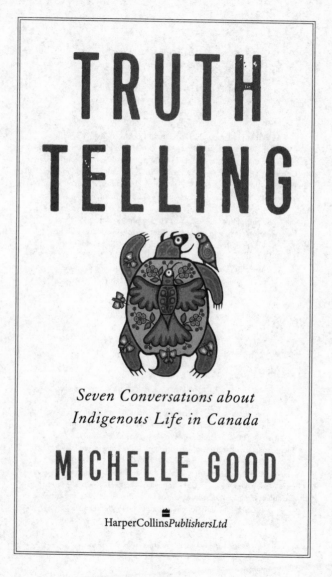

*Seven Conversations about
Indigenous Life in Canada*

MICHELLE GOOD

HarperCollins*PublishersLtd*

Published by HarperCollins Publishers Ltd

First edition

An earlier version of "Racism, Carefully Sown" called "A Tradition
of Violence" was published in *Keetsahnak: Our Missing and Murdered Indigenous
Sisters*, edited by Kim Anderson, Maria Campbell, and Christi Belcourt. Published
by University of Alberta Press, 2018. An earlier version of "Cultural Pillagers" was
published in the *Globe and Mail* ("'Play Indians' Inflict Real Harm on Indigenous
People," May 21, 2021) and appears in the collection *Best Canadian Essays* 2023.

HarperCollins books may be purchased for educational, business or
sales promotional use through our Special Markets Department.

HarperCollins Publishers Ltd
Bay Adelaide Centre, East Tower
22 Adelaide Street West, 41st Floor
Toronto, Ontario, Canada, M5H 4E3

www.harpercollins.ca

Library and Archives Canada Cataloguing in Publication

Title: Truth telling : seven conversations about Indigenous life
in Canada / Michelle Good. | Names: Good, Michelle, author.
Description: Includes bibliographical references.
Identifiers: Canadiana (print) 20230168477 | Canadiana (ebook) 20230168515
ISBN 9781443467810 (hardcover) | ISBN 9781443467834 (EPUB)
Subjects: LCSH: Indigenous peoples—Canada. | LCSH: Indigenous peoples—
Canada—Social conditions. | LCSH: Indigenous peoples—Canada—Government
relations. | LCSH: Indigenous peoples—Canada—Social life and customs.
LCSH: Canada—Race relations. | LCSH: Reconciliation.
Classification: LCC E78.C2 G66 2023 | DDC 305.897/071—dc23

Printed and bound in the United States of America
23 24 25 26 27 LBC 5 4 3 2 1

For my Jay

When one lives in a society where people can no longer rely on the institutions to tell them the truth, the truth must come from culture and art.
—JOHN TRUDELL

CONTENTS

||||||||

TRUTH TELLING

SIT WITH ME,
BY THIS DIALOGUE FIRE

||||||||

A T THE WATERSHED MOMENT IN CANADIAN history when the Truth and Reconciliation report was issued, the Honourable Justice Murray Sinclair positioned truth as mandatory and a precedent for reconciliation, articulating the fundamental principle that without truth there can be no reconciliation.[1] This phrase has become like an anthem in the raised voices of Indigenous and non-Indigenous people alike. The urgent demand for truth has become a Call to Action in itself. The problem with anthems, though, is that they tend to become rote like an absent-minded genuflection, a premeditated land acknowledgement, reduced to the sound of the words without mindful consideration or intention to follow through. These public gestures are simply a tipping of the hat without any commitment toward substantive recognition of the rights of Indigenous Peoples to implement jurisdiction in our territories.

Truth is more than fact. In Canada, truth must be unearthed from beneath the myth of Canadian history. That history must be understood in a deeply contextual way if we are to move beyond positional and confrontational relationships and into functional ones dedicated to substantive change. We must step away from the window dressing of reconciliation.

We must come to a place of understanding that the colonial history of Canada was genocidal in nature, functioning as an imperative embedded in the very heart of colonialism.

The conversations, academic and otherwise, about colonialism articulate its complexity and we see work in its derivatives: postcolonialism, neocolonialism, settler colonialism, and so on. Each of these iterations, and more, generate important and elucidative study. At the same time, I find, it distracts from the fundamental meaning of colonialism, and it is critical that its ugly heart not be lost in the study of it. Colonialism is:

> *The policy or practice of acquiring full or partial political control over another country, occupying it with settlers, and exploiting it economically.*[2]

That's it. That's all. This is the unvarnished, grasping truth of the intention of colonizing European nations that set their sights on the riches of the so-called New World. Human settlement was only secondary to the economic goal. The colonizing settlers are simply the drones in the beehive of colonial ventures; their value limited to how well they enrich the various states who financed the colonial venture.

I often visualize what I refer to as the "colonial toolkit": a collection of implements used to activate the aims of colonialism. All the implements in the toolkit were, and are, employed to remove us from our lands, disempower us in decisions about our lands and resources, dismantle our highly effective social institutions, and dismember our families and communities. To accomplish these colonial goals, there were, for example, policies established that mandated the starvation of Indigenous Peoples to force their submission. To dismantle traditional family structures, social institutions, and community systems, we saw policy and law mandating the wholesale removal of children for placement in residential schools, for the sole purpose of deconstructing them and reconstructing them in the image of white men.

To understand the brutal circumstances Indigenous Peoples of Turtle Island continue to endure, we must reach under the myth of Canadian history. We must embrace history in the way Indigenous Peoples experienced it as it *truly* unfolded. Only then will non-Indigenous Canadians begin to grasp the true horror of what we were subjected to and how the seeds of that horror continue to sprout and take hold in our lives today.

It is also important to understand that history does not only refer to events almost lost to the mists of time. History is also contemporary. Contextually, the history of relations between Indigenous Peoples and those who settled here must be understood in the context of first contact but also in times as recent as last year. The history of Indigenous/non-Indigenous relations is on a continuum from the beginning to now and must be understood that way if non-Indigenous Canadians are ever to grasp what the prerequisites to substantive reconciliation in fact are. To participate meaningfully in reconciliation, non-Indigenous Canadians must not only be supportive but must also insist that the resources (natural, political, and financial) required for substantive change are generously and enthusiastically provided as needed and articulated by Indigenous Peoples. Non-Indigenous Canadians must use their privilege to leverage *real* change. It is simply not enough to wear an orange shirt or issue empty land acknowledgements. The non-Indigenous population of this country must not only talk, they must also act.

These are not academic essays, neither are they exhaustive. They are my personal take on this new world brought to us by colonialism; a world in which we still struggle to survive. These essays examine the brutal intentions of colonialism that continue to harm us, whether that be in the form of starvation policies, residential schools and their child welfare descendants, the acceptance of brutality against our women, the dishonesty of government, or the insufficiency of monetary compensation.

I encourage readers to start with the first essay as it provides a historical foundation that informs the subsequent essays.

I also encourage readers to consider Indigenous reality in the true context of these histories to deepen their understanding and call upon their own compassion and responsibility to engage in these conversations beyond the last page.

During momentous occasions, many Indigenous people engage in the ceremonial practice of lighting a spirit fire to engage the Ancestors, so to speak. The fire remains burning, day and night, until the occasion is complete. These essays are intended to spark dialogue; to provide a deeper view of both early and contemporary history through the lens of Indigenous experience. Let us, together, light a dialogue fire. Let us keep the flame alive until truth overturns the colonial lie.

Camp North of Indian Camp
rifle-pits

June 2nd 1885

Big Bear!
I have utterly defeated Riel, at
Batoche with great loss, and have
made Prisoners of Riel, Poundmaker,
and his principal chiefs, also the two
murderers of Payne, and Tremont, and
I expect that you will come in with all
your prisoners, your principal chiefs,
and give up the men, who have com=
=mitted murders at Frog Lake, (and I
am glad to hear that you have treated
them fairly well) If you do not, I shall
pursue & destroy you, and your band,
or drive you into the woods to starve,

Fred. Middleton
M Genml

RESIDENTIAL SCHOOLS

||||||||

The Coup de Grâce of a Canadian Genocide

WHILE THE DEEPENING TRUTH ABOUT RESIdential schools is finally slowly working its way into the Canadian consciousness, there is still a conceptual gap that prevents an understanding of the whole, unlaundered truth. There are still people who believe that residential schools were a well-intentioned venture gone wrong; an effort to educate and prepare Indigenous people for a changing world. There are still so many people, particularly those who hold the reins of power, who fail to see residential schools as part of the colonial effort to assert political control over this land, occupy it with settlers, and exploit it economically. The imperial push of Britain and other European nations was not to find lands that would offer a new home built with respect and care. Quite the contrary, North America was seen as a cash cow with only one major obstacle standing in the way of exploiting it economically, the Indigenous Peoples who lived on these lands. So, there was a drive to decimate the Indigenous population, ancient civilizations, complete with their own well-established, very successful economies, in order to give their land to settlers who, in turn, would feed the new capitalist economy. Traditional Indigenous economies were fundamentally different and provided for subsistence. Exploitation of resources for surplus, that is, for profit, was an alien concept to Indigenous Peoples. So was the colonial use of violence, including taking Indigenous women hostage until their men agreed to trap for profit, or confiscating their rifles, leaving them unable to provide and protect, to force their cooperation by other means.[3]

The residential school initiative was not the first colonial strike against the Indigenous Peoples of this land. In 1670, long before the decision to establish these institutions and mandate Indigenous attendance, King Charles II of England stole what was known as Rupert's Land (the Hudson Bay watershed) and gifted it to the Hudson's Bay Company (HBC). There was absolutely no consideration granted to the Indigenous occupants of that territory in this transaction. Immersed in the self-serving notion of the Doctrine of Discovery and its partner, the concept of *terra nullius* (meaning "nobody's land"), England claimed Rupert's Land and, in the interests of cashing in on the fur trade, gave it away as though they owned it. In 1889, two years after Confederation and under pressure from England, the HBC reluctantly sold Rupert's Land to Canada for $1.5 million, which is equivalent to $31,710,000 in 2022 dollars. The sale of this land was a huge financial fraud perpetrated against the Indigenous Peoples of those territories. This is not only about the outright theft of lands and resources, it's also about how the colonizers alienated Indigenous populations from the natural resources that had provided for them for thousands of years. Acquiring Rupert's Land was critical in the context of western expansion and Canada's economic future. Without Rupert's Land, Canada would be limited to the northeast corner of the continent and would be cut off from tapping into the rich resources of the Prairies and the valuable agricultural land needed to attract new immigrants, who, in turn, would populate the region and fuel the economy. For these reasons, obtaining the territory in question was a top priority for the Dominion government once Confederation had been achieved. Less than a year following Confederation, negotiations for the purchase of Rupert's Land commenced between Britain and the HBC, which ultimately relinquished its charter to Rupert's Land. Full control was then transferred to Canada under the *Rupert's Land Act* of 1868 and the Northwest Territories Transfer Act of 1870. Once again, this transaction occurred without consideration of the interests of Indigenous Peoples. With these pieces of legislation, the Dominion now considered itself to have extended its jurisdiction over the Northwest Territories

(NWT) and proceeded to develop administrative structures and provisions for the application and enforcement of Canadian law and jurisdiction in those territories. However, before they could do this, as required by the terms of transfer, Canada was obligated to resolve all Indigenous claims to the land, as outlined in the October 7, 1763, Royal Proclamation of King George III, which stated that:

> *Whereas it is just and reasonable, and essential to our Interest and the Security of our Colonies, that the several Nations or Tribes of Indians, with whom We are connected, and who live under our Protection, should not be molested or disturbed in the Possession of such Parts of Our Dominions and Territories as, not having been ceded to, or purchased by Us, are reserved to them, or any of them, as their Hunting Grounds.[4]*

This acknowledgement from the Crown that unceded Indigenous territory belonged to Indigenous Peoples is, in fact, recognition that Indigenous

Peoples retained jurisdiction in their unceded territories.

Using the Robinson Treaties as a template, the Crown, through its colonial government, began negotiating with the Indigenous Peoples. It is important to understand that treaty-making was not new to Indigenous Peoples. For hundreds of years before European encroachment on North America, treaties were struck between various Indigenous groups to establish relationships with each other and mutual agreements about the shared use of territories. This historic use of treaties is important to acknowledge because the Indigenous Peoples undertook treaty-making in good faith with the full expectation that the Crown would also be acting in good faith and would give full effect to the terms of the treaties. It's also important to understand the historic backdrop to this time of treaty-making.

In the decades leading up to the aforementioned time of treaty-making, Indigenous Peoples were faced with not only the encroachment of settlers in their territories, but the destruction of their economies by the intentional slaughter of the buffalo. In the US and Canada, the buffalo were slaughtered for their hides. Often, whole carcasses were left to rot after the tongue, popular in the cuisine of the day, was removed. This slaughter was encouraged by both the American and Canadian governments and was yet another implement in the colonial toolkit. Since the buffalo were critical to the survival of the Plains people, the decimation of the herds was an intentional strike against their ability to provide for themselves, a strike against self-sufficiency. The buffalo were a sacred gift to the people, providing them with food, clothing, and shelter. The wholesale slaughter was devastating to the people, not only because of the resulting impoverishment and starvation, but also because of the horror of such wanton destruction of the Creator's gifts.

With the decimation of the majestic herds that roamed the North American prairies, Indigenous people became vulnerable through this intentional impoverishment. Sir John A. Macdonald rigorously followed "a policy of submission shaped by a policy of starvation."[5] Promised rations were with-held not only to reduce costs but to disempower people through starvation. The story of Chief Big Bear (Mistahimaskwa) at Frog Lake perfectly exemplifies the pressure exerted upon Indigenous Peoples to enter into treaties that were far more favourable to settlers and the state than they were for them.

Despite the decimation of their traditional economy, Big Bear resisted taking treaty for six hardscrabble years, during which time his Band experienced extreme hardship through starvation, disease, and harassment as the Crown pressured them to surrender their rights. But Big Bear was determined to achieve a better deal for his people than what was being offered. He knew the treaty was unfair and weighted in favour of settlers. Finally, in December 1882, under extreme duress brought on by his Band's desperate circumstances, Big Bear had no other choice but to enter into treaty. However, he refused to choose a reserve, describing the reserve system as a noose around the neck of his people. Three years later, when the Crown failed miserably to live up to its treaty promises and the members of Big Bear's Band were literally starving to death, the younger men of the Band rose up against the Indian agent who was withholding their rations. Frog Lake erupted in violence and the Indian agent, a priest, and others were killed.

The North West Mounted Police, also known as the Canadian Militia, was then dispatched to capture and arrest Big Bear and members of his Band. Skirmishes between the Band and the militia occurred over the next months with Big Bear defeating the militia at Frenchman's Butte, after which the militia hounded Big Bear's Band through the Cypress Hills and into Montana. To understand Canada's intention, one need only read correspondence from General Middleton, commander of the militia, who ordered Big Bear to surrender or he would "pursue and destroy you and your Band or drive you into woods to starve."[6] Big Bear ultimately surrendered at Fort Carlton on July 2, 1885, three months after the incident at Frog Lake. He was charged with treason and sentenced to three years' incarceration at Stony Mountain Penitentiary. He served half of his sentence and then was released, due to severe illness. He lived for another year and a half with his daughter on the Little Pine Reserve, where he died and was buried.

Just as there is a mistaken notion that residential schools are from an era long ago, the history of conflict between colonial Canada and Indigenous Peoples is also thought of as a situation from the distant past. This erroneous thinking was recently brought home to me when my mother's last remaining sibling, my Auntie Margaret, passed away in the fall of 2021, not long after her ninety-eighth birthday. I visited the graveyard at Red Pheasant to pay my respects. While there, I visited with other family resting places, including my grandparents' graves. It hit me in that moment that my grandfather was born only seven years after the Frog Lake incident, and his mother, in all likelihood, was there, given that she was a close relation of and member of Big Bear's band. This places the military assault subsequent to Frog Lake squarely in the living memory of my family. To truly understand the trauma wrought by warfare against Indigenous Peoples in this country, it is imperative that people recognize such violence as a part of very recent history.

The imbalance of power and the desperate circumstances of the Indigenous Peoples of the Plains allowed the Crown to prevail with wholly insufficient treaty terms and left Indigenous people without recourse when these terms were not fulfilled.

Eleven of the numbered treaties were negotiated between 1871 and 1921. Like some of the earlier treaties, these western treaties included so-called civilizing clauses that encompassed education and provisions for a transition from a hunting and gathering way of life to an agrarian one. The Dominion, through the terms of the treaties, was to support this transition with the provision of training, farming implements, and livestock. The government placed farm instructors on reserves who were imbued with great power over the daily lives of Indigenous people. Not surprisingly, despite Indigenous interest in developing farming skills, two terminal obstacles were placed in their way. First, the Dominion government failed to live up to its obligations with respect to the development of Indigenous agriculture. Supplies and equipment were not provided in sufficient amounts or in a timely way. For example, the Bands were only to receive one plow per ten families. Settler farmers on the Prairies believed that the terms of the treaties, promising necessary implements and supplies for farming, were given as charity. They failed to grasp that these goods were to be provided in return for the agreement of Indigenous Peoples to share land that was rightfully Indigenous land, as acknowledged by the Crown and the colonial government. Non-Indigenous settlers also believed that such provisions (no matter how woefully inadequate) gave Indigenous farmers an unfair advantage in farming. Settler farmers believed that the provisions provided through treaty were on an enormous scale and that, with such huge subsidies, reserve farmers would be able to undersell non-Indigenous farmers. This could not be further from the truth. However, rather than educating settlers about the terms of the treaties and explaining that provisions to Indigenous farmers were modest and in return for permitting white settlers to establish their homes on Indigenous land, the government impeded Indigenous farmers with obstacles that made it virtually impossible for them to succeed.

In 1889, the federal government imposed the Peasant Farming Policy, which was nothing more than a series of limitations for Indigenous farmers, implemented to placate the non-Indigenous settlers. Indigenous farmers were ordered to cease producing wheat and to grow root vegetables and other grains only. They were also prevented from using modern farming equipment and required to make any implements they needed themselves. They could only seed by hand, harvest with scythes, bind by hand, thresh with flails, and grind grain with hand mills. This policy was in place until 1900.

In addition to starvation policies, the destruction of the traditional economy, deliberate deprivation, and ignoring the terms of treaty, the spiritual underpinnings of Indigenous life were also targeted by the colonial machine. On the Prairies, the Sundance and other ceremonies were made illegal, and Indigenous people were punished for praying in the ways they had for time out of mind. But this was more than just punishment; it was a further attack on the integrity of Indigenous culture and society. Such laws were an intentional effort to destroy Indigenous culture, including the spiritual identity and healing powers of traditional ceremony.

Likewise, the traditional governing institutions were officially undermined by the provisions of the *Indian Act* that defined how leaders would be elected and what the limits of their authority would be. A quick review of the powers of elected Chiefs and Councils as articulated in the *Indian Act* demonstrates how complex and effective traditional governing institutions were replaced with Councils with far less authority than municipalities. A perfect example is the Potlatch Law of 1885. The Potlatch, through an amendment to the *Indian Act,* was made illegal because it was seen as anti-Christian. The Potlatch is an ingenious, ancient institution that formed the economic structure of some Indigenous societies and governed the management of resources through the passing down of names, which were imbued with responsibilities for the management of territories and resources associated with those names. The Potlatch ban was not lifted until 1951.

During this time, residential schools were already operating. The Mohawk Institute opened in 1831 (and closed in 1970). However, attendance at residential schools was low, and so in 1920, the federal government made attendance at the schools mandatory. The *Indian Act* was amended to reflect that attendance was required, and the *Act*'s regulations laid out penalties in the form of fines and incarceration for parents who refused to send their children.

These legislated acts of colonial violence were aimed directly at eradicating Indigenous independence, economic self-sufficiency, social and governing structures, cultural norms, spiritual practices, and family and community cohesion through the large-scale kidnapping of the children. During the parliamentary debates surrounding the proposal to make attendance at residential schools mandatory, and to give priority to them over community-based schools, Sir John A. Macdonald explained his support of residential schools by saying: "When the school is on the reserve, the child lives with his parents who are savages; he is surrounded by savages . . . he is simply a savage who can read and write."[7]

It is clear that this agenda of the colonial, Dominion, and federal governments of Canada was to undermine and terminate the very existence of Indigenous Peoples in their own land. Many, including the Government of Canada, have stated that the objective of residential schools was to assimilate the children and to promote their integration into non-Indigenous society. They offer this explanation as a sort of *mea culpa*, as though they are admitting something terrible. But, again, they are neither accurate nor truthful in this assertion.

Following the Second World War, Winston Churchill referred to the Jewish Holocaust as a "crime without a name." In response to this inability to find language that would reflect the intent and scope of crimes of that magnitude, Raphael Lemkin coined the term *genocide,* which was created by combining the Greek word γένος (*genos,* "race, people") with the Latin suffix *caedo* ("act of killing"). Genocide is the intentional destruction of a people, usually defined as an ethnic, national, racial, or religious group. With the term, an articulation of acts that constitute genocide was developed, and is as follows:

- killing members of the group
- causing serious bodily or mental harm to members of the group
- deliberately inflicting on the group conditions of life calculated to bring about its physical destruction in whole or in part
- imposing measures intended to prevent births within the group
- forcibly transferring children of the group to another group

Virtually every type of genocidal act articulated by the Genocide Convention is an accurate description of the colonial violence that was done to Indigenous Peoples, the impacts of which are not limited to the colonial period. The acts themselves continue today with the wholesale apprehension of Indigenous children by child welfare services and the continued murder of Indigenous women on a scale entirely disproportionate to other murder statistics. These are just two examples of the ongoing reality of modern-day colonial violence.

Taking a long and in-depth look at the history of relations between Indigenous Peoples and the Canadian state is the only way that one can truly see how the colonial period was a relentless, genocidal, and violent campaign against the people who sprung from this land. So why have the oft-touted measures taken by successive governments failed to address the ongoing social inequity that arose from this colonial endeavour? Because these objectives of termination remain intact, if not explicitly, then implicitly. They lurk in the structural systems of government, industry, and society. Until those systems change fundamentally to reflect acceptance of Indigenous jurisdiction and the right to Indigenous self-determination and self-government as designed by Indigenous Peoples, and not bureaucrats locked into systems born of colonial thinking and approaches, the dynamics of the oppressor and the oppressed will remain, and the suffering of, and theft from, Indigenous Peoples will continue.

The late twentieth and early twenty-first centuries have been the age of the apology. The Protestant churches started offering apologies for the residential schools in the early 1990s. The federal government, after numerous refusals, finally offered an apology in 2008, but only because the vastly insufficient settlement agreement could not be finalized without an apology. Most recently, in Rome, the Pope offered a conditional apology, still not apologizing on behalf of the church itself but instead on behalf of some of its members. While these apologies do provide comfort for some, they are entirely symbolic and wholly insufficient. Considering this concerted and genocidal effort to annihilate us, how can empty words possibly be adequate? These apologies are nothing more than an attempt to buttress ecclesiastical piety and political favour. And indeed, the words are empty. The federal government's apology issued by then Prime Minister Harper preceded the completion of the Truth and Reconciliation Commission's (TRC) report with its ninety-four Calls to Action. The Calls to Action articulate an impressive range of systemic change required to restore Indigenous Nations to a position of independence and self-determination. Just as those non-Indigenous farmers perceived compensation as charity, non-Indigenous Canadians tend to view the implementation of the TRC as a charitable act instead of seeing it as the righting of massive historical wrongdoing.

Canadians must stop viewing history through a colonial lens. Canada, this supposed place of freedom and democracy, is a myth. The story of how Canada was created is a fairy tale with little basis in truth. And this faux history continues to be spoon-fed to Canadian children who become the newest beneficiaries of a false narrative about their country. These children then grow into adults who carry on the fallacies necessary to maintain the foundation that perpetuates a grossly disproportionate power dynamic. This is why change and progress continue to be slow.

More and more, we hear the refrain that there can be no reconciliation without truth. When we say truth is called for, prayed for, and so desperately needed, we are not just asking for the acknowledgement that the residential schools existed and harmed so many innocent children. The truth that is needed is that this Canadian genocide happened and continues to happen. Only when people understand and admit to the depth of the violence and injustice levelled against Indigenous Peoples will there be an impetus to promote and support structural change and a willingness to embrace a new Canada, one that actively restructures itself to accommodate Indigenous jurisdiction and self-determination. Ironically, on October 27, 2022, the House of Commons unanimously approved a motion put forth by Indigenous MP Leah Gazan recognizing that the residential school endeavour was in fact a genocide. Just a few months later, the

Winnipeg Police Service refused to search a landfill for the remains of Indigenous women murdered by a serial killer, despite the fact they knew the remains were there. So, while the House of Commons performs its acknowledgement of genocide, the systems of government continue to reflect the violence and disregard inherent in colonial values. The casually articulated decision to leave these women with the garbage reinforces the long-held belief that not only are Indigenous women disposable, but the need of their families to bring them home and take care of them in a good way is insignificant and unimportant.

Let the age of the apology end. We don't need any more apologies. We need an acknowledgement of the harm that's been done. We need a *mea culpa*, followed by full and proper restitution.

Most recently, the Supreme Court of Canada (SCC) dismissed the appeal of survivors of the notorious St. Anne's Residential School. This institution, some will remember, used a homemade electric chair to punish children or torture them just for the entertainment of their jailers. The SCC did not even respect the survivors enough to provide reasons for its refusal to hear them. It is difficult to remain optimistic when, once again, the law interferes with justice. Once again, violence against Indigenous people is seen as acceptable. How can we believe in reconciliation in the face of such quietly violent disregard? However, persist we must.

LUCY AND THE FOOTBALL

||||||||

ONE THING I WILL SAY ABOUT INDIGENOUS Peoples is we have mastered the art of maintaining hope. Through the brutalities of hundreds of years of colonialism, now firmly entrenched in the social fabric of this country and weaponized against us, we remain. Against all odds, we keep on hoping that the promises will stop being empty, that the apologies will be more than symbolic, that Lucy will not pull that football away at the last second, and that Charlie Brown won't go flying, again. We are still standing and still advocating for the change necessary for Canada to make sufficient room for our Nations to restore themselves to a state of self-determination socially, politically, and economically. This is a heavy burden we bear, as Lucy repeatedly makes her promises and we fall flat on our backs, again, as she snaps the football away at the last minute, again.

Reconciliation is not a state of mind, an attitude, or a well-meaning commentary, although those things are necessary to lay the groundwork for setting things right. But the process must not stop there. Perhaps this is why the TRC did not create a list of things to think about and discuss earnestly over tea at the book club. Instead, they articulated Calls to Action, outlining very specific and concrete changes that need to be undertaken to move us all along the path to reconciliation. Yet, seven years later, we remain bogged down endlessly talking about what reconciliation means as the Calls to Action gather dust just as the recommendations in the 1996 Royal Commission on Aboriginal Peoples remain largely unfulfilled. Indigenous Peoples have never stopped articulating what is needed for our return to a self-determining state. We have, through activism, legal advocacy, social education, and protest, brought to light, in a multiplicity of ways, over many decades, the kinds of social restructuring that is necessary for our people to have peace and prosperity in our own lands. Setting things right is reconciliation. More comprehensively, reconciliation necessitates structural societal change, right down to the roots. And of course, what we find at the roots is the rot of the colonial imperative.

What I mean by the colonial imperative is the drive to achieve political control of a territory for the purpose of exploiting it economically. This imperative is grounded in the Doctrine of Discovery issued by the Catholic Church in 1452 as its emissaries sought out the riches of "new" lands. The Doctrine of Discovery implores followers to:

> *Invade, search out, capture, vanquish and subdue all Saracens and pagans whatsoever and other enemies of Christ whatsoever placed and the Kingdoms and dukedoms, principalities, dominions, possessions, and all moveable and immoveable goods what-*

soever held and possessed by them and to
reduce their persons to perpetual slavery, and
to apply and appropriate to himself and his
successors the kingdoms, dukedoms, counties,
principalities, dominions, possessions and
goods, and to convert them to his and their
use and profit.[8]

One must consider the complete hegemony of the Catholic Church at the time. The Church ruled the Old World and gave carte blanche to invaders to destroy everything Indigenous for "their use and profit."

Hand in hand with the Doctrine of Discovery is the principle of *terra nullius,* a term that refers to a "territory without a master."[9] It is used in public international law to describe a territory that is inhabited but does not belong to an identified state, meaning the land is not owned by a recognized state. In fact, when a state or an entity describes a land as *terra nullius*, the land is, in reality, occupied, by a Nation or Nations, usually Indigenous Peoples, but the term has been another enabling legal

concept used to legitimize foreign state occupation and colonization.

The foundation of legal and political institutions in this country arises from these doctrines, which are imbued with the overall objective to control and subjugate Indigenous Peoples and banish them from their land in order for the colonizers to profit from the resources of the land unimpeded by the rights of the original peoples. This is the truth Canadians resist: that the systems we unconsciously and uncritically accept are riddled through and through with oppressive, discriminatory, and exclusionary structures underpinned by deeply held beliefs that portray Indigenous Peoples and our systems as inferior. These structures, as part of the colonial imperative, are what spawned the policies that resulted in the criminalization of so many aspects of Indigenous life, from spirituality to self-governance to raising and educating our own children in our own communities. Residential schools did not arise from a well-meant initiative run amok. Even the most basic research reveals the destructive intent at the foundation of their design

and implementation. They were not schools. They were institutions akin to the re-education centres of the Cultural Revolution in China and its current re-programming camps where ethnic Uyghurs are detained.

The purpose of reconciliation in the context of the TRC's work was to establish the imperatives for restoring or creating a healthy and respectful relationship between Indigenous Peoples and non-Indigenous people. The Calls to Action, which arise from the information and analysis collected in the report itself, call for the structural changes necessary for Indigenous Peoples to cast off the bonds of colonialism and exist side by side with non-Indigenous Canadians as mutually respectful equals. This was the understanding between Europeans and Indigenous Peoples during the earliest days of contact as represented in the Treaty of the Two Row Wampum and all subsequent treaties.

In 1613, Mohawk people observed Dutch settlers moving into their territory and clearing land for settlement. A delegation was sent to meet these newcomers, and they negotiated the terms of how

the two groups would interact with one another. It is said that the Dutch suggested the Mohawk refer to them as "father." The Mohawk, wanting a relationship term that would more effectively indicate a relationship of equals, chose the term *brother* instead. The agreement between the Haudenosaunee and the Dutch is recorded through beads on a Wampum Belt. The Two Row Wampum Belt depicts two boats navigating a river independently of each other. It was meant to represent a relationship of equality and mutual respect. The Belt consists of two white rows against a purple background representing the river of life. One row symbolizes the Haudenosaunee as an autonomous people with their own law and customs, while the other represents the Europeans. Never do the two rows overlap and this is meant to convey that the parties to the agreement would live peaceably and independently of each other, as equals. Nearly 150 years later, in 1764, the year after the Royal Proclamation of 1763, the terms of that treaty were reaffirmed at the Treaty of Niagara, where more than two thousand Chiefs from twenty-four Nations met to extend the Covenant Chain of Friendship, a multi-nation alliance between Indigenous Nations and the British Crown. The Treaty of the Two Row Wampum was read at the gathering to further establish the importance and ongoing standing of the agreement it represents. The proceedings included a reading of the Royal Proclamation of 1763, which places a duty upon the Crown to engage in treaty-making with Indigenous Peoples and wherein King George III expressly forbade the taking of Indigenous lands without agreement and compensation.

So, from the earliest days, Indigenous Peoples were absolutely clear in their intent to continue their lives in the manner they always had. They negotiated what they understood to be treaties with the newcomers, the terms of which proclaimed their sovereignty and were binding in perpetuity. Through these treaties, the newcomers became allies. When the myth of Canada is taught and reinforced endlessly, reference to the critical role the Indigenous allies played in the wars between the French and the English is little more than a footnote, if it's included at all. These Indigenous allies were instrumental in the establishment of the geographical boundaries that ultimately would represent the map of Canada. These early treaties generated a sense of loyalty in the Indigenous Peoples, and the same loyalty was expected in return. Instead, the European settlers offered betrayal upon betrayal of the Indigenous parties to treaty.

Instead of maintaining the terms of those early treaties that would have allowed for the mutual prosperity and social wellness of both Canada and the Indigenous signatories, Canada wasted no time in abrogating the terms of the treaties. To abrogate means to repeal or do away with a law, right, or formal agreement. It also means evading a duty or responsibility. The treaties with the Indigenous Peoples of the Prairies are a particularly good example of this, although I don't think the obligations born of any treaty in Canada have been upheld. For example, Treaty 6, which covers a significant swath of the Prairies, promised assistance in the transition from the hunter-gatherer lifestyle to an agrarian one, given the intentional decimation of the buffalo. Indigenous people died in droves during the years leading up to and subsequent to the formalization of these treaties. Starvation and poverty were widespread thanks to the colonial destruction wreaked on the traditional economies. Starvation policies were, in fact, formalized by the government of Sir John A. Macdonald.

I think of Chief Big Bear and his great reluctance to enter into treaty, feeling it would be a noose around the neck of his people. I think of the desperation that led him to finally relent at Fort Walsh. Almost immediately, after entering into treaty, the terms of that treaty were broken by Canada. In 1885, violence broke out at Frog Lake due to Canada's abject failure to follow through on the terms the parties had agreed to. Indigenous people were still starving despite the promises embodied in treaty. Rations were not provided, the resources promised to support a transition to an agrarian lifestyle fell far short of what was needed and promised, and policies such as the Peasant Farming Policy were put in place to intentionally undermine the ability of Indigenous people to prosper in the economy Canada itself had laid out for them as an imperative alternative to their traditional economy.

The fact that the foundational truth of the early relations between Indigenous Peoples and settlers is not taught in schools contributes to the failure of non-Indigenous people to truly grasp the legally binding nature of these treaties. The truth has been subsumed into the myth of Canada. Instead, for more than two hundred years, the powers that be have woven an alternative story of a benevolent Canada, one determined to save the poor Indians. It is painfully ironic that the only saving we needed was precipitated by the colonial violence that reduced us to paupers in our own land. In its creation myth, Canada has become a master at obfuscating the truth of racism, greed, and colonial hunger for power and economic and political dominance over Indigenous Peoples. Nonetheless, despite its best efforts, Canada has not been able to eradicate us or our legally binding rights.

When Pierre Elliott Trudeau was prime minister, there was a major transition in the struggle for recognition of Indigenous rights. Trudeau was deeply opposed to distinct status for Indigenous Peoples and in 1969 presented a White Paper proposing the elimination of Indian Status in Canada. This was a direct strike against the collective nature of First Nations and would have seen the elimination of all Indigenous rights, and reserve lands would have been parcelled out as private property. Indigenous Peoples across the country rose up in such a fierce way that the proposed legislation was tabled. The exceptionally diligent and well-organized resistance to the termination inherent in the White Paper is a nod to the power and determination of Indigenous Peoples that it would be this same termination-oriented prime minister who would ultimately preside over the Constitutional Amendment of 1982 that saw the inclusion of Aboriginal rights in the Constitution via Section 35, which says:

The existing aboriginal and treaty rights of the aboriginal peoples of Canada are hereby recognized and affirmed. (2) In this Act, "aboriginal peoples of Canada" includes the Indian, Inuit and Métis peoples of Canada.[10]

To go from the proposed termination of all Indigenous rights to the elevation and reassertion of them as a part of the Constitution was not a gift from the assimilationist Trudeau government. No, this change was the result of the powerful activism of Indigenous Peoples. The recognition of Aboriginal and treaty rights as Constitutional rights was a time of great celebration for Indigenous Peoples across the country, and in particular for activists and advocates who had dedicated their lives to seeing Indigenous rights recognized in the new Constitution as these same rights had been in the *British North America Act*, Canada's original Constitution. The Constitution is the supreme law of the land, and no non-constitutional law may conflict with it. Neither can Constitutional rights be amended or changed without following the amending formula, which itself is a part of the Constitution.

Once again, Lucy stood with the football in hand, promising us that finally the rights entrenched in our treaties and other agreements would be more clearly articulated in the new Constitution and recognized in such a way that we could exercise those rights in our drive to a return to self-determination. These newly articulated Constitutional rights would be the leaping-off point. Finally, we could stop resisting the ongoing colonial efforts to destroy us because our rights were now unequivocally a part of the supreme law of the land. We could now focus on rebuilding our Nations in a relationship of equals with Canada.

Now, forty years later, are we there yet?

In my view, the entrenchment of Aboriginal rights in the *Constitution Act* was a moment of great opportunity for Canada. It was then that we should have seen a return of lands, the negotiation of resource-sharing agreements, and the end of government interference in Indigenous governance. That time should have been the starting point of the restoration of Indigenous self-determination. Once again, however, Lucy pulled the football away, again, and again and again, this time using the Supreme Court of Canada to define the scope and meaning of Section 35 rights. Somehow, for the Indigenous population, the supreme law became less supreme.

In 1984, the leadership of the Gitxsan and Wet'suwet'en people filed a claim against the Government of British Columbia to establish their jurisdiction over 58,000 kilometres of lands and waters in their traditional territory in north-western BC. After twelve years of wending its way through the courts, from the BC Supreme Court to the BC Court of Appeal, it finally landed before the Supreme Court of Canada. In its landmark 1996 decision in *Delgamuukw*, the Supreme Court of Canada established a test for determining whether a Nation held Aboriginal Title to its traditional lands. That test required the Indigenous party to demonstrate occupation of the land in question prior to the assertion of Crown sovereignty, that there was no break in the continuity of Indigenous occupation of said territory between the time before the assertion of Crown sovereignty and the present, and exclusive occupation by the Nation claiming title. Importantly, the Supreme Court also decided that Aboriginal Title is a collective right and one that goes beyond the right to engage in traditional uses of the land. Critically, the court found that, in the context of the Gitxsan and Wet'suwet'en peoples, Aboriginal Title had not been extinguished.

Twenty years later, in 2014, the SCC recognized that the Tsilhqot'in people held Aboriginal Title to 1,750 square kilometres of traditional territory in the province of British Columbia. Aside from the declaration of Aboriginal Title, this decision was important as it held that Indigenous occupation did not have to demonstrate the establishment of a permanent village but could also be bound up in other historical Indigenous practices, such as seasonal migration or management of hunting, fishing, or trading rights. In these ways, an Indigenous community's Aboriginal Title may apply to an extensive territory. However, in the next breath, the court found that Aboriginal Title does not negate the Crown's sovereign title to the land. Rather, Aboriginal Title is defined by the court as a burden on that title, much like a modern-day lien registered against land title. And so, again, we are left with a failure to truly recognize Aboriginal Title as an exclusive and unextinguished right to the land. Likewise, the proviso implements a limitation that falls far short of restoring the relationship of equals as established through the treaties noted above. The spirit of the agreements between Indigenous Peoples and the settlers was once again an unequal one, with Canada declaring itself as the dominant partner.

But, could there have been a different outcome? Could the Supreme Court of Canada, the ultimate Canadian legal institution, make a finding that was fundamentally against itself? This is a perfect example of how Indigenous rights are thwarted by the power structures of Canada. These claims to Aboriginal Title should never have been before the SCC. If we acknowledge the nationhood of the parties to the treaties, how can the institution of one nation make a determination against the rights of another? An international court should have heard these cases, and then there would have been at least a chance that the relationship and agreements would have been determined to have been made between equals and upheld as such. The impact of this inability of Canada to rule against Canada is that the supreme law as articulated in Section 35 of the *Constitution Act* is not seen as applicable when it comes to Aboriginal Title. A perfect example, of course, is the matter of the Wet'suwet'en people. The SCC explicitly found that they retained title to their territories. Yet, when Wet'suwet'en people resist the construction of a pipeline on their traditional territories, they are criminalized by paramilitary forces just as Big Bear's Band was criminalized for resisting treaty and then for demanding the terms of treaty be met. Time and again, the courts have found against the Wet'suwet'en people on this matter, which begs the question, how can a Canadian institution rule against Canada in such a fundamental issue as land title? The rule of law, the rule of the supreme law, apparently, cannot be relied on by Indigenous parties because the courts are Canadian institutions bound by laws infused with colonial objectives and assertions of ultimate Crown sovereignty. In a word, the courts are stacked against us.

So, when we consider the question of reconciliation in light of the real history of relations between

Indigenous Peoples and Canada, it becomes a far more complex issue with a far more complex trail forward.

Indigenous Peoples are often characterized as parasitic on the state. This is not new. In the 1890s, Indigenous farmers were prospering despite the failure of the Crown to provide farming implements as promised in treaty. White prairie farmers raised such a hue and cry arguing that Indigenous farmers were being given an unfair advantage that the Crown responded by implementing the Peasant Farming Policy, which denied Indigenous farmers the use of mechanized farming equipment and limited the types of crops they were permitted to grow, among other things. Just recently, I observed a comment responding to a news story in which Indigenous Peoples were expressing their disappointment with the Pope's visit. The person who commented said, "nothing is ever enough [for Indigenous people]." It made me think of those white prairie farmers who considered treaty payments as charity and successfully demanded that the government hobble Indigenous efforts to make a transition to an agrarian life. From those very early days, Canadians bought into the myth of Canada as the benevolent provider to Indigenous Peoples as opposed to the colonial oppressor determined to control the valuable resources on Indigenous lands. It is Indigenous Peoples who are, in fact, the benefactors of Canada. It is what was stolen from us that has sustained this country from day one.

The main challenge to achieving meaningful and substantive reconciliation is the generations of Canadians who have been weaned on the false history of Canada and now hold tight to that which is simply not true. As a judge stated when admonishing far-right radio show host Alex Jones in his recent high-profile court case in the US, "Just because you claim to think something is true does not make it true."

Once again, it is Indigenous Peoples who are at the vanguard, defending themselves by insisting on truth and raising awareness about their centuries of mistreatment in this country. The discovery of unmarked graves at residential schools across

Canada sent shock waves through the country. Although Indigenous people have always known about the massive death rates in these institutions, it is a fact that has been suppressed since the early 1900s, and the pressure to keep this knowledge out of the public eye has been immense. But now that Canada has been forced to accept this truth, it's created a compelling opportunity to reconsider the true history of Canada. Yet, how heartbreaking that it took the deaths of these wee children (and decades of denial of their deaths) to make Canadians finally question their indoctrination.

The need to recharacterize Canadian history is a prerequisite of reconciliation. There needs to be a willingness to allow the truth of Indigenous reality to surface, and Canadians must face it, internalize it, and only then can we truly consider and chart the best way forward. As the TRC wrote:

> *Without truth, justice, and healing, there can be no genuine reconciliation. Reconciliation is not about "closing a sad chapter of Canada's past," but about opening new healing pathways*

of reconciliation that are forged in truth and justice. We are mindful that knowing the truth about what happened in residential schools in and of itself does not necessarily lead to reconciliation. Yet, the importance of truth telling in its own right should not be underestimated; it restores the human dignity of victims of violence and calls governments and citizens to account. Without truth, justice is not served, healing cannot happen, and there can be no genuine reconciliation between Aboriginal and non-Aboriginal peoples in Canada.[11]

Reconciliation must be preceded by the acknowledgement of the truth. How can things be put right if Canada is still failing to acknowledge the deep truth of its ongoing attacks on Indigenous Peoples? The process of making things right, as they were originally meant to be, is the challenge Canada and its citizens face when it commits to reconciliation. This simply cannot happen until we all recognize the truth and commit to a new day.

Canada must not only acknowledge the truth of the harms that have been inflicted on Indigenous Peoples, it must also atone for the causes of that harm and commit to action that will change the structural behaviour that led to these harms in the first place. This requires dismantling systems that are incapable of rendering just solutions and revisioning them as inclusive and representative of both Indigenous and non-Indigenous aspirations. Non-Indigenous Canadians need to understand that their circumstances will change if we are to achieve reconciliation. We cannot create balance without a redistribution of wealth and power. Indigenous Nations simply cannot achieve self-determination if these old power dynamics are not radically changed.

Creating and holding space for Indigenous Peoples to correct history and impart the truth is a non-negotiable prerequisite to reconciliation. We don't just want Lucy to hold firm to that football instead of pulling it away. We want her to set aside her need to control the ball, and instead, with truth as our foundation and goodwill our mandate, we'd like her to stand with us as equal partners to build a road forward based on mutual acceptance of our respective nationhood. Then, and only then, will reconciliation be possible.

RACISM, CAREFULLY SOWN

||||||||

I T WAS 1949 WHEN MY FATHER SHARED HIS plans to marry my mother with his family. They would wed in late summer. My grandmother's reaction was disappointing, to say the least. She took to her bed for days and swore my father would be disowned if he followed through; that his choice of a wife was a disgrace and would bring the family into disrepute. My grandmother's response had nothing to do with my mother's character or conduct. In fact, at the time, my mother was a bit of a celebrity, feted in the national press upon her return from New Zealand, where she had trained as a nurse and a midwife. This and her other accomplishments would have been extraordinary for any Canadian woman in the 1940s but so much more for my Cree mother. At the age of nine, she was forced to leave her family at the Red Pheasant Indian Reserve to attend the St. Barnabas Indian Residential School in Onion Lake, Saskatchewan. She was subjected to many of the brutalities that are commonly known to have occurred in those institutions. They certainly were not schools. She spoke no English when she arrived at St. Barnabas and so would have been punished for speaking Cree until she could pick up enough English words to get by. She spoke of always being hungry and the terrible food; the slurs that were thrown at her and, tragically, watching her friend Lily hemorrhage to death on the playground from advanced tuberculosis. The little girl was one of the thousands who died alone and far from home. The government was well aware of the extreme death rates associated with the rampant spread of tuberculosis in the institutions as their own study, conducted by Dr. Peter Henderson Bryce, confirmed and condemned the deplorable conditions and the resulting death rates. Nonetheless, Canada refused to make the necessary changes to stem the tide of tuberculosis infection, knowing full well the children were dying at rates as high as 50 per cent in some schools.

There was a violence inherent in the colonial framework of these institutions. Young girls were targeted in many ways, with particular emphasis on undermining their sense of themselves as eventually taking their rightful places in the matriarchy of their communities. When my mother refused to eat tainted food, she was made to sit for hours upon hours on a hard chair in the dining room, being told she would sit there until she ate the food. So, there she sat until it became clear to her jailers that she would not bend to their will. So instead, she was dragged before the principal, who was quick to tell her she was "nothing but an Indian slut and would never be anything but an Indian slut." She was eleven years old. Since the earliest days of colonization, this sexually charged characterization of Indigenous women was a carefully curated one. The story of Pocahontas is a prime example.

Settler Americans have re-characterized this story as a love story. That could not be further from the truth. A child when she first met John Smith, Pocahontas helped him obtain a rudimentary ability in her language while she also learned English. She assisted Smith in his negotiations about the land and where he was permitted to settle. Although Pocahontas was only twelve years old, artistic representations of her at the time portray this child as a highly sexualized adult woman. She was depicted as a princess, which both objectified her and presented her in a way that made other Native Americans seem less civilized.

The principal's response to my mother's defiance was to silence, demean, and disempower her. His weapon of choice was to resort to a derogatory, sexualized attack on her character. This careful creation of Indigenous women as lustful sexual objects was well established by the time my father shared his plans to marry an Indigenous woman. Shock and horror were the predictable responses from my non-Indigenous grandmother, stemming from a conditioned racist and derogatory understanding of what it meant to be an Indigenous woman.

I often wonder what made my mother rise up so furiously, to accomplish things so beyond the reach of an Indigenous woman in Canada in the 1940s. But rise she did. Having been raised as a self-respecting person in our Cree ways, perhaps it was the outrage she felt at her treatment at St. Barnabas that inspired her wild dreams. My mother, like so many children, contracted tuberculosis in the institution. Treatment was rudimentary in the 1930s, and she was subjected to forced bed rest for three years in the St. Michaels' Sanatorium in Prince Albert, Saskatchewan. She would have had so much time to think; time to dream, and for a plan to take shape. She wrote letters endlessly, looking for a way to get an education at a time when training beyond the ninth grade was prohibited for Indigenous Peoples in Canada. Upon her release, she somehow managed to find some support and won a scholarship to train with the Canadian Mothercraft Society in Toronto. Upon completion of the program, she was hired by a wealthy family in Toronto as a nanny. Her world opened up with that job. The family took her everywhere with them, including such unlikely destinations, for a little Rez girl, as New York City, San Francisco, and Bermuda. It was another scholarship that took her to New Zealand for three years to train as a nurse and a midwife. Upon her return to Canada, she was inundated with offers from various universities, each accompanied by a full scholarship. She was thirty years old at this point, an accomplished, worldly, and educated woman. She had risen up against the odds of her circumstances and attained the benchmarks in a life that distinguish a person and imbue them with credentials worthy of respect.

But none of this mattered to my grandmother. All that mattered was that my mother was Cree, and any children from the union with my father would be even worse. They would be "half breeds." After my parents married, my grandmother continued to torment my mother. During my mother's first pregnancy, my grandmother invited her to tea with her lady friends and announced her preg-

nancy by stating that my mother was "having pup-
pies." She never missed an opportunity to degrade
my mother and shame my father for marrying her.

Back then, as it still is now, racism was rampant in Saskatchewan. It's difficult for me to think
about how so many people felt the impact of this
hatefulness. My mother's situation was playing out
in 1949, against the backdrop of the end of the Second World War, the role of Canadians in liberating
survivors of the Holocaust still fresh in the collective consciousness. These were heady days when
notions of human rights were gaining international momentum through the League of Nations
and, ultimately, the establishment of the United
Nations. *Never Again* carried a promise of a better
world, an inclusive world. Paris, December 1948,
and the lofty language of the Universal Declaration of Human Rights rang out, lifting people up,
asking them to insist on a world where *All human
beings are born free and equal in dignity and rights.*[12]
How could my mother have been treated this
way at a time when the world was railing against
intolerance and racial hatred? Was it because my

grandmother was a monster? Was her racism unusual? No. Sadly, she was a Canadian prairie woman of her time. Her attitudes, prejudices, and outright social brutality were the culmination of generations of conditioning that led to attitudes that only the most agile and critical mind could escape. Her parents, grandparents, and great-grandparents were settlers, and if not active participants in the violent subjugation of Indigenous Peoples, they were certainly passive observers. Even the most well-meaning people of the time would have had to find a way to justify this hateful behaviour toward Indigenous people, which they knew was inhumane and contrary to any notion of human dignity.

In the 1920s, the Ku Klux Klan (KKK) took hold in Canada, but nowhere like it did in Saskatchewan. By the late 1920s, the membership in the KKK was over 25,000 people, which represented almost 4 per cent of the population of the province. Saskatchewan also bears the dubious honour of having been represented in Parliament by the treasurer of its chapter of the KKK. Walter Davy Cowan served as mayor of Regina and served as the Conservative-Unionist member of Parliament for Regina from 1917 to 1921 and then as Conservative MP for Long Lake from 1930 to 1934. To be a member of the KKK you had to be white, gentile, and Protestant. While the Canadian KKK was not limited to Saskatchewan, the views of this group dominated the politics of the day, just as my mother was trying to make a life for herself in Saskatchewan. I can only imagine the fear and anxiety she must have experienced trying to navigate her biracial marriage in such a racist environment.

It's so difficult to understand how successive generations of settlers reconciled the emerging notions of human and civil rights with the deep racism that justified the brutality they visited on my ancestors. To create a place for themselves in this land, the settlers accepted the belief that success necessitated the exploitation and destruction of Indigenous Peoples. I do not believe that these people were inhuman, but for people to act with such violent inhumanity, a justification is required. Violence without justification is indefensible. And so, just as our own people are blamed in politics and society for the murder and disappearance of thousands of Indigenous women and girls, those in power during the days of aggressive, violent settlement created an image of Indigenous women that justified our treatment as chattel. That image developed into a worldview that has been conveyed with a terrible efficiency over time. When pressed, people cannot say why they believe the things they believe about Indigenous women. Through the everyday commentary of everyday citizens, this view of Indigenous women has proliferated and become entrenched in the collective subconscious of Canada, rendering Indigenous women disposable in the eyes of modern Canadian society.

"Happiness is but a dream for Canada because the malice that has marked so much of human history happened here too,"[13] says Professor James Daschuk in his arresting analysis of the role of disease and the politics of starvation in disenfranchising the Indigenous Peoples of Canada. In *Clearing the Plains*, Daschuk provides a meticulously researched analysis of how Indigenous women were reduced to items of ransom and barter as their families struggled with the horrors of a manufactured famine, which was intentionally created to establish economic supremacy for the newcomers and the subjugation of Indigenous Peoples.

In the context of the vicious competition between Britain and Canada for supremacy in the fur trade, a horrifying brutality was routinely perpetrated against Indigenous women by officers of the Crown and condoned by those in power. The control of Indigenous populations and their transformation into indentured servants in the fur trade was critical to the quest for dominance in the fur trade. As Daschuk notes in his work:

> *Canadian traders (vs. the British Traders of the HBC) soon found ways to overcome the Chipewyan aversion to commercial trapping. By the early 1790s they routinely took women from their families to ensure payments of debts and sold them to company employees . . . "If the father or Husband or any of them resist the only satisfaction they get is a beating and*

they are frequently not satisfied with taking the Woman but their Gun and Tent likewise," wrote scandalized HBC surveyor Philip Turner. *The chief Canadian trader along the Mackenzie, Duncan Livingston, was highly regarded by his peers. Under his management these people were modeled anew and brought under an implicit obedience to the white's authority. NWC post master Willard Wentzel wrote to Roderick Mackenzie. That "authority" in the Athabasca included a slave traffic in women.*[14]

To achieve the compliance of the men and secure their participation in enriching the settlers through the fur trade, some women were held hostage, and worse. We must understand and acknowledge that this was not just the conduct of some rogue fur traders. This attack on Indigenous women was a weapon in the colonial toolkit that was used right into the second half of the twentieth century, and, arguably, it continues to this day.

Daschuk notes that the "sexual improprieties

of DIA (Department of Indian Affairs) employees" were widespread and well known by their superiors.[15] Forty-five per cent of government officials living in the then Northwest Territories were known to be engaged in predatory relations with young Indigenous girls, contrary to their stated mandate of being a moral example. Not only did these predatory relations cause great pain and havoc for Indigenous Peoples, but they also contributed to the escalation of violence against predatory Indian agents for which Indigenous people paid a heavy price. Referring to the so-called Frog Lake Massacre, Daschuk writes:

> *Twenty-six years after the killings, fur-trader-turned-missionary Jack Matheson provided a more sinister motive for the violence . . . "An Indian girl more or less didn't matter; and I've seen ration cards held back six months till girls of 13 were handed over to that . . . brute"* (the Indian Agent). *One of the killers at Frog Lake, Wandering Spirit, had spent eighteen months in prison for assaulting another DIA*

employee, John Delaney. While he was incarcerated, Delaney "took his girl wife."[16]

Daschuk also notes that, in addition to being taken hostage and held as sex slaves, Indigenous women were forced into a form of prostitution when rations were withheld unless they provided sexual favours to the Indian agents:

> *Contrary to S.W. Hurrell's assertion that prostitution came to the North West Territories as sex workers moved west with the railway, prostitution among aboriginal women was a survival strategy resulting from the poverty experienced in their reserve communities after the disappearance of the bison.*

The desperation of starvation forced Indigenous women into this "sex for food" trade instigated by DIA employees, forcing them into a form of human trafficking.

In another instance, John Norrish, the farm instructor for the Blackfoot reserve, was engaged in a practice of withholding and trading rations for sex. It was discovered that he was buying sex with flour when certain women on the reserve had bogus ration cards, provided by him, that gave them three extra rations of flour. It was believed within the Department of Indian Affairs that the women were not willing participants in this growing food-for-sex form of institutionalized predation. So, in response to the widespread "scandal over the traffic of Indian women involving DIA employees,"[17] the *Indian Act* was amended in 1886 to make Indigenous women prostitutes subject to prosecution. It was reported to Parliament that girls as young as thirteen were being sold to white men in the West for as little as ten dollars. Hector Langevin MP, now proudly remembered as a Father of Confederation, rejected the notion that Indigenous girls and women were being trafficked, asserting that "to Indians, marriage is simply a bargain and sale, that the parents of a young woman are always on the alert to find a buyer for her."[18] Langevin was an MP in the mid- to late-1800s, once again demonstrating that these were not events that happened hundreds of years ago. These beliefs and behaviours are in the living memory of our people. They are also in the living memories of the descendants of the Fathers of Confederation.

Likewise, it is well known that Hayter Reed, a strong proponent of the control and subjugation of Indigenous Peoples and who initiated the Pass System that made it unlawful for Indigenous people to leave the reserve without the permission of the Indian agent, took a young girl from the Touchwood Hills as his "mistress" and that she bore him a child. Rather than being censured, he was promoted to the role of Indian Commissioner and played a key role in the development of Indian Residential Schools and in the government's stubborn refusal to respond in any way to the concerns about sexual abuse, disease, and starvation in those schools.

Daschuk's research is invaluable because it outlines in horrific detail the methods that were employed in the process of subjugating and dehumanizing Indigenous people in the name of settling the West. The legacy of this dark chapter of colonialism is that Indigenous women are still seen as disposable, as a commodity to be used by members of the non-Indigenous community as they see fit.

The role of "word of mouth" in the creation and perpetuation of the negative stereotypes that plague the lives of Indigenous women was an idea that first came to me while I was teaching as a sessional history instructor. I was teaching a year-long history unit on Indigenous people in Canada. As any Indigenous person knows, that "story" is not our story. So, out of a desire to inspire my students, and to challenge their preconceptions, I asked them in a group discussion to share what they "knew" about Indigenous people in Canada. I sat there, listening to all the tired, old stereotypes rolling out of the mouths of these young people like memorized nursery rhymes. And it hit me. They *are,* in a hideous sort of way, memorized nursery rhymes. I thought about all those childhood rhymes and folk songs: "I See London, I See France," or "Ring around the Rosy." How do we come to know these chants? Ask yourself, *Where DID I learn that?* I feel pretty confident that you will not, with spec-ificity, be able to say where you learned this. So, I took things a little further and asked them, *Now, how do you know these things to be true?* To their credit, they were aghast. They could not at first even speculate about how they had come to know and hold as true the deeply racist stereotypes they had internalized. Slowly their assumptions started to unravel. My dad told me. My grandfather used to live next to a reserve and he told me. My auntie, my mother, my grandmother said. Always, invari-ably, the source of the "information" was familial.

So, then I turn my thoughts to the likes of Hector Langevin, Hayter Reed, Duncan Camp-bell Scott, and every other non-Indigenous person, and think about the things their children over-heard them say as well as the things they would have actively taught their children to justify the way Indigenous people were (and still are) treated in this country. Generation upon generation of non-Indigenous Canadians have been weaned on racism and bigotry and, rather than nurturing acceptance and respect, a bedrock of centuries-old disgust and disregard informs the social conception and treatment of Indigenous women in Canada. Indigenous women are disposable, objects to be used and discarded. Indigenous women are less than human and can be treated as such.

It took years and years for the chorus of voices demanding an inquiry into the thousands of missing and murdered Indigenous women in Canada to be successful. We heard for years that one of the factors leading to the demise of these women was the assumption that they lived high-risk lifestyles such as working in the sex trade. This was a common reason for rejecting pleas for an inquiry. Even if this were true, does it justify a failure to protect them or properly investigate their deaths? It was only after the doctoral research of Maryanne Pearce demonstrated that, in fact, only a very small percentage of these murdered women were involved in the sex trade that an entirely new public perspective began to emerge. Rather than sex workers who contributed to their own fate, these were young girls, students, teachers, mothers, daughters, and sisters from all walks of life. Contrary to the assumptions reinforced by the government and media, these women represented a cross section of the female Indigenous population. So how is it that media, politicians, police, and the public at large automatically assumed that these women had endangered themselves through participation in the sex trade? Even when releasing the report handed down by the RCMP in which they acknowledged the numbers of missing and murdered Indigenous women, an RCMP representative once again voiced this myth that these women had put themselves in harm's way. Granted, the only information about the victims reported to the public at the sensational media trial of Robert Pickton, and the less prominent media coverage of John Martin Crawford, was that those particular women worked in the sex trade. But there is something deeper afoot.

The legacy of the men (founding fathers, bureaucrats, and company men) who reduced our women to disposable goods can be found in virtually every stratum of society. Indigenous women live our lives in a state of fear that we might be next on the list of the missing or murdered. All the while, the country glorifies the likes of Hector Langevin (yes, the same Langevin for whom the building housing the Prime Minister's Office and the Privy Council was named, until very recently) and Hayter Reed, a sexual predator and one of the architects of the Pass System, the Peasant Farming Policy, and residential schools. It's easier to understand how our women came to be perceived as disposable when we imagine how these prominent men brutalized our women as a strategy in the subjugation of a people. The same men who are glorified for their contributions to Canada in our history books.

The practice of ignoring the deaths and disappearances of Indigenous women is rooted in the history of colonialism. As Daschuk notes, the killing of Europeans was widely publicized in the media at the time and continues to be a focal point in the broader historical examination of various so-called uprisings in Canadian history. The murder of Indigenous people during these conflicts or during this time of great upheaval received scant attention at the time. And the failure of the media to report on the wholesale murder of Indigenous women today is reflective of their history of maintaining an illusionary image of both Canada and Indigenous people. In *Seeing Red: A History of Natives in Canadian Newspapers*, the authors provide a careful analysis of the media in Canada and suggest that:

> *Insofar as the content of newspaper imagery derives from the larger culture in which its readers participate, one might reasonably expect a consonance between press content and pre-existing reader bias, the result is that the news constitutes a kind of national curriculum, which emerges organically as if nothing were more natural. In short, as curriculum news, images do not present new material so much as they simply reinforce the status quo.*[19]

The writers conclude that colonial archetypes and behaviours have become essentialized so that wildly inaccurate ideas about Indigenous Peoples have become normalized and form a kind of

Canadian "common sense," one that informs reactions to issues as devastating as the disappearance and murder of thousands of Indigenous women. Rather than sparking an urgent sense of something terrible happening over and over again that must be addressed, and operating out of this carefully contrived national mindset, media reports elicit "nothing more than tsk tsks and knowing nods of the head."[20] Those tsk tsks are a shorthand for a complex colonial curriculum that, if anything, culminates in the oft-reported notion that these women brought this violence onto themselves.

In addition to the random violence against individual Indigenous women, there is another form of institutionalized violence that strikes at the very heart of Indigenous matriarchy. I refer to the long history of Indigenous women being subjected to forced sterilizations in Canada. For decades, many Indigenous women have been subjected to tubal ligations without their consent and, often, despite their explicit refusal to provide consent, and in yet other cases, without their knowledge. Indigenous women have reported coercive tactics such as threats to report them post-partum to child welfare if they did not consent, which in most cases would result in the apprehension of newborns.

Under Section B and D of Article II of the Genocide Convention, genocidal acts include "causing serious bodily or mental harm to members of the group" and the imposition of "measures intended to prevent births within the group," all with the intent to destroy an entire group or population.

Consider the foundation of colonialism, the Doctrine of Discovery. This Catholic decree, issued in the form of papal bulls, deemed lands inhabited for centuries by Indigenous Peoples as *terra nullius*. This is a legal finding that a land is considered unpopulated on the basis that the peoples living there were not Christian, in particular, Catholic. Those populations were deemed subhuman and, therefore, their territories could simply be taken. For me, the Doctrine is the foundation of colonialism because it allowed the Indigenous Peoples of Turtle Island to be deemed less than human, allowed for the wholesale appropriation of lands, and established a position of superiority and authority in white Christians over Indigenous Peoples. This sense of superiority is reflected in all colonial policy, and the harm created continues to ripple through the lives of Indigenous people.

I think about my grandmother again and the way she equated my mother to a dog and, by extension, the way all Indigenous women were seen in this light. What do those in control of female dogs do? They spay them. The forced sterilization of Indigenous women was undertaken with the same belief that to do so was the right and purview of the state-run medical system.

Recently, at least one class action lawsuit by Indigenous women who were subjected to forced sterilization has been launched. Likewise, the Senate began studying the issue in 2019 and put forward Bill S-250, which would see the criminalization of forced or coerced sterilization. Under the current criminal code, forced or coerced sterilization could be the basis for a charge of assault, but the Senate decided to categorize it as its own form of crime carrying a maximum sentence on conviction of fourteen years.

This practice of forced sterilization is yet another example of the devastating attack on the Indigenous matriarchy aimed at the depopulation of Indigenous Peoples.

During the formation of Canada as we know it today, the degradation of Indigenous women was entrenched in the national sensibility. Is it any wonder that less than a hundred years later, my grandmother would be horrified at the prospect of a Cree daughter-in-law? Someone educated my grandmother to think of Indigenous women as less than human. At the same time, her entire generation, and the one before it and after it, received what I think of as a form of oral history, passed down from one generation to the next, perpetrating these ideas so effectively that 155 years after Confederation, these negative images are still superimposed on our women. These damaging ideas about Indigenous women are killing us, like a permission slip for rape and murder.

Non-Indigenous populations of Canada would be well advised to take a page from the book of those Indigenous groups who argued at law that oral history must be given equal weight to written history. First in the decision in *Delgamuukw v. British Columbia* [1997] 1010 and later in *Squamish Indian Band v. Canada* (2001 FCT 480) and *R. v. Ironeagle* (2000 2 CLNR 163), the courts began to recognize the legitimacy of the modalities of our way of keeping history.

In our struggles for recognition of our rights, we fought for the recognition of oral history at law. In the arguments we made to the courts, what the mainstream saw as our "myths" and superstitions were presented as cogent histories of our peoples. These arguments formed a foundation for the recognition at law that information is transferred orally from one generation to the next. Our value systems and social structures were conveyed through our oral traditions. I believe that the same thing, though structurally different, is true for non-Indigenous Canada. The way of spoken traditions passing from one generation to another is not exclusive to us and, in fact, played a key role in passing this tradition of bigotry, hatred, and violence from colonial to postcolonial Canada.

The values of the colonial era have been perpetuated through an oral tradition, bolstered by the media and the blatant (or thinly veiled) racism that underlies government policy.

The triumvirate of media as curriculum, government policy, and oral history colludes to make it exceptionally difficult to deconstruct this carefully curated and devastatingly wrong perception of Indigenous women. This must, however, be done if we are to end the profound violence against our women.

There is so much work to be done to combat the generations of inaccuracy and erroneous ideas about Indigenous women. For decades, we have demonstrated artistically, intellectually, culturally, politically, and socially that our ways of life, social structures, cultures, and spiritual beliefs are sophisticated and entirely contrary to the proliferative and brutish Canadian mainstream depiction of Indigenous women. And yet, it is an image Canadian society still stubbornly refuses to relinquish. Indigenous women remain locked in a mirror with a false reflection, created by political and social forces. Why has Canada failed so miserably in correcting this erroneous sense of who Indigenous women really are? In my view, the influence of the founding fathers was deeply successful in promulgating the idea of Indigenous women as unimportant and worthless to their own communities, much less having any value in the non-Indigenous community. This negative idea is deeply entrenched in the fabric of this country and has been conditioned into Canadian society since those horrific times when we were being starved out of our homelands.

It is only when I look through this lens that I am able to understand how it is that my grandmother would be so shaken to her core at the prospect of my mother joining her family. It was conditioned into her and those generations before and after her, as thoroughly as the words to "O Canada."

The horrors perpetrated against Indigenous women in Canada, with what can only be described as a silent acceptance by government and society alike, stem from these deeply held beliefs. Increasing policing and government programs and teaching women how to be safe is not going to correct this situation. Only understanding and a commit-ment to telling the truth about the cruelty inflicted on our women in the name of settling this country would help change people's perceptions, end their complacency, and stop the continued brutalization and dehumanization of our women.

Canada must know the truth of our history. Now that the door is starting to open and the truth of Indian Residential Schools as a life-and-death experience is finally coming to light, the treatment of Indigenous women throughout our history must be recognized and acknowledged if we ever expect to be treated with the respect and dignity we deserve.

$13.69

||||||||

THIS PAST WEEK, I RECEIVED THE FINAL instalment of my Sixties Scoop compensation. Given the number of people accepted into the class action, the compensation per person amounted to $25,000. With so much time and distance between me and those terrible years in care, I can look back and consider that experience through the eyes of an adult. I was in care for five years with six different placements in that time frame. I did the math. This compensation works out to $13.69 per day in government custody. Memories of some of those days rise to the surface and I wonder, who might think that any one of them could be properly compensated by thirteen dollars and sixty-nine cents?

How about the day the man who was supposed to be my counsellor terrorized me in a swimming pool at a government facility and then, when I ran away from him, sexually assaulted me in the women's change room? Does $13.69 make that day bearable in my memory? Or the day, not long after being made a ward of the province, when I wrote a letter begging to be returned home because the teenage son in the family where I was staying was terrorizing and sexually harassing me? Does $13.69 make that easier to cope with? No one ever replied to that letter. Years later, I got a copy of my child welfare file through freedom of information and that letter was there among the various documents. I was thirteen years old when I wrote it and had completely forgotten about it. I was forty-five years old when I requested my file and when I saw that letter it broke my heart. Even though I thought I was pretty grown up when I wrote it, I was still such a child, referring to my mother as *mommy*. Reading those documents, I wept for her, that child, feeling the stinging silence of no reply, no help, no intervention. I attempted suicide for the first time when it became clear no help was on the way. If nothing else, that got me out of that nightmarish place and away from that boy, who would ultimately obtain a professional designation and face disciplinary proceedings for his continued sexual improprieties. I was sent to a "receiving home," which is a kind of stopover between placements. I remember it so well despite the fact I was only there for a few days. The woman running it was so gentle and kind and for once I felt safe. But, almost immediately, I was sent to another place where children were being exploited regularly. I often think of a girl who was there with me. Her name was Lucienne. One of the people in charge ended up taking off with her and making her his common-law wife. She was fourteen. I still think of Lucienne and wonder what ever became of her. In one placement, my bedroom was a pantry closet with an accordion door and no window. I had this little portable stereo; where I got it or how, I don't remember. Listening to Joni Mitchell was my sanity until I was told to turn off "that noise." Another placement saw me sleeping in a dingy, dank basement along with three other foster kids. We were fed one menu, while the foster parents and their kids had an entirely different one. I still hate chili, something we were served almost daily. In all but one of those "homes" there was virtually no supervision. I came and went as I pleased. No one cared where I was or what I did so long as the cheque arrived each month.

My family lived in northwestern British Columbia, and I was in foster homes in Vancouver. This was the early 1970s and people didn't travel as routinely as they do now. As a result, I very rarely saw my family. My youngest sibling was about ten years old when I was made a ward of the provincial government. As a result, I never really had a relationship with her. My relationship with my older brother also all but ended when I went into care. Shortly after I left the family, he began what would be a highly successful military career. My older sister was in university in Vancouver for part of the time I was in care, but I never saw her. I broke my

leg very badly when I was fifteen and was hospi-
talized for almost six months. I was in traction and
entirely bedridden for the whole time. My foster
parents came to visit twice, as I recall. My parents
did not come at all. My older sister came once in
the first week. It was a nice visit. She helped me
eat my dinner. My best friend had a terrible phobia
of hospitals, but she overcame it to visit me once.
That visit meant the world to me. Her own childhood trauma was related to hospitals, and I knew
how difficult it was for her to overcome her deep
aversion to being there. But she did, and she did it
for me. I could have died of loneliness. Instead, I
read. If it were not for books, I don't know how I
would have survived those endless days, flat on my
back. I turned sixteen in the hospital. There was
nothing very sweet about it.

I knew I was depressed even before the added
struggle of that hospitalization. The depth of my
despair was so overwhelming that it manifested
in physical symptoms. Imagine walking through
the world as though you are surrounded by a deep,
damp fog. That's what it felt like. I thought of

suicide almost every day. After I was released from the hospital, I began a campaign for permission to live on my own. I successfully negotiated this with my social worker and found myself a one-room studio apartment with a kitchenette and a shared bathroom. It was down on Main Street in Vancouver, before Main Street was cool. It was a dangerous place back then. Social Services paid the rent directly to the landlord, and I received a food voucher for about a hundred bucks each month. The IGA grocery store just down the road was one of the few places that would give me my change in cash after I bought a little food; otherwise, I would have had nothing for bus fare or smokes.

While the apartment was a total dump, to me it was the most wonderful place. The relief I felt was almost immediate. Freedom. It was like an antidote. Escaping the oppressiveness of foster care, I was now on a path of my own choosing. I started an upgrading course and was introduced to Canadian literature in my English class. I fell in love with the works of Margaret Laurence, Ethel Wilson, Margaret Atwood, and Alice Munro, among others. I was so moved by Maria Campbell's *Halfbreed* and George Ryga's *The Ecstasy of Rita Joe* and had an intuitively deeper understanding of those books than my white classmates. My emotional response to both works compounded a sense of otherness in me that was, nonetheless, motivating. With an already well-established journalling habit, I began experimenting with poetry, and my love for the written word grew along with my dreams of one day being a writer myself. The time I spent studying Canadian literature was a reprieve, an escape, from my struggle to cope with sexual trauma, the loss of my family, and the overwhelming sense that I was not worthy of love or care. Everything had been taken from me. I am well aware of how the trajectory of my life was flattened; how emotional and psychological injury, and the resulting anxiety disorder, created barriers to success throughout the years. Even now, I struggle with these impacts, though less. I work hard at not thinking of what my life might have been had I not been so profoundly interfered with. There is simply no point to it. Still, I wonder.

Every day I was in care, my ability to trust eroded, and my sense of myself as someone without value, someone unworthy of love, safety, or encouragement, settled into my bones. But, to my great fortune, not long after I aged out of foster care, I met Chief George Manuel. It was at a public meeting, and I was deeply impressed with his impassioned speech. I was there with a friend who was also a speaker and I insisted that my friend introduce me to him. George shook my hand, and I told him I wanted to do the kind of work he was doing. He told me to drop by the Union of BC Indian Chiefs' offices sometime, and so I did. I realized in hindsight he was not saying *Come to the office and we'll have a meeting*. Rather, it was a polite response to a kid. George was not there when I dropped in, but I was told his son Bobby was and he would meet with me. I laugh remembering that I sat in reception for over three hours, reading, with Bobby sticking his head out quizzically every now and again. I just figured he was busy, not that he had no idea who this white-looking girl was and what she wanted. He did meet with me though, and despite his misgivings, he contracted me to write a paper on child development. This would be the first of many jobs I held with First Nations and Indigenous organizations before I went to law school in 1996. Becoming a lawyer fulfilled a childhood dream as well as a desire to sharpen my skills and, therefore, my ability to advocate for Indigenous people in a different way.

I found shelter and meaning in working with other Indigenous people and it became my life's work. It was not without its complexity and trials, but it was meaningful work: a cause, a reason to strive. It also opened a pathway that helped nourish a deep hunger in me to understand my own Cree heritage.

In the '70s, trauma was not something anyone talked about. It was not a part of a larger, public conversation, as it is these days. I had never even heard the term *post-traumatic stress disorder* (PTSD), other than in the context of war veterans. Even that conversation was more often than not about shell shock as it related to the World Wars and Vietnam. Understanding the profound damage and life-changing impact of childhood trauma just wasn't a part of the world, at least not my world. No one questioned my sudden and intense behavioural changes. Before I was made a ward, and even after, no one wondered why.

For some reason, and this is certainly not unique to me, I thought it was my fault that I was raped just two months after my thirteenth birthday. I was so deeply ashamed that I was entirely unable to tell a soul what happened. Instead, some of my textbook responses to trauma told the story. Running away, rebellion, anger, fear, a deep desire for someone to understand and help make it better, undermined by a certainty that no one could possibly help, because after all, it was my fault. I was a walking disaster, without the maturity or insight to see a road through it all. How could I have had either? I was a child.

The extreme physiological changes that are precipitated by trauma, notably changes in the composition of body chemistry and a sharp increase in production of the fight-or-flight hormone cortisol, leave an indelible mark on the abused child. Without any kind of therapeutic intervention, trauma responses just become a person's way of being in the world. All people see is the victim of trauma over-reacting to most everything. Being fearful or rageful or tearful; making illogical choices that seem like the only choice and only reinforce oneself as blameworthy; or just generally being out of sync with "normal" people. For so many years, I lived my life in a defensive stance, putting up a fight when the only thing I was fighting was my own suffering and the fear that someone would find their way through the armour, to the very tender soul I always was, and destroy me all over again.

In the 2000s, I was working for a small law firm when five residential school cases were referred to me. I had only recently been called to the bar at the age of forty-four, but I resolved those cases very successfully. However, I did not understand why I was always in a state of deep sadness, or was easily triggered, filled with anxiety, and overwhelmed by depression as I worked my way through those files. It was those cases that triggered an awareness in me that I was still a deeply traumatized person in need of some help. I got a referral to an excellent therapist, and I am so thankful to him to this day. I was devastated to receive a diagnosis of complex, chronic life-long PTSD complicated by major depressive disorder. This explained some tensions at work, at least, to me. I went to speak with the man in charge and disclosed my diagnosis, hoping it would contextualize some of those workplace difficulties. His response was to lash out at me, retorting, "Well, we didn't do it to you," followed by a lengthy diatribe basically about the many ways I was irritating to him. Needless to say, I didn't stay there long. I didn't stay anywhere long until I established my own little law firm, creating my own comfort zone, my own place of belonging.

I was so fortunate to have found a milieu, both before and after law school, that gave me not only meaningful work but, ultimately, a meaningful life as well.

This is not how life usually pans out for kids in care. More typically, the lives of young people aging out of care are characterized by poor mental and physical health, addictions, low academic achievement, eating disorders, homelessness, un-employment or underemployment, shortened life expectancy, conflict with the law, early and often single parenthood, an inability to maintain healthy relationships, and deep alienation and loneliness.

I experienced many of those things as well and, in some ways, still do, living a deeply sol-itary life. I was once a delightful little girl with the whole world in front of me. I was bright. I loved singing. My kindergarten teacher taped my singing voice once and sent it to her brother who was the music consultant at the University of Denmark. He responded saying he'd never heard such control and promise in such a young voice. I loved reading and devoured everything I could, reading well beyond my years at an early age. I read Rachel Carson's groundbreaking book *Silent Spring,* a non-fiction plea about the impact of pes-ticides on birds, when I was eleven years old. I was a driven child.

I remember in grade four there was a school assembly coming up, and our class was doing a musical number, a song about a ballerina. The girls were to try out for the role of the dancer. I was not in dance lessons. But, oh, I wanted to be that ballerina! So, I went to the library and looked at as many pictures of ballerinas as I could put my hands on. I remember the black-and-white pictures of those graceful women. I practised the poses I saw, imagined them with music, and danced my little heart out at our auditions. I was chosen over the other little girls who actually *were* in ballet classes. After the performance, their mothers asked mine who my teacher was. I guess that was the beginning of a long life of being largely self-taught. I thought everyone was a good person. I loved my siblings and my parents with all my heart. I completely believed that my life would unfold with meaningful and loving friendships. I wanted to get married and have a bunch of kids. I wanted to be a lawyer. I wanted to be a writer. I figured one day for sure, despite dreaming it in a little company town in northern BC, I would meet the Beatles. I had prospects. All of that was taken from me. What was left was a thin shadow of all that was ever shiny and hopeful about me.

Yet, somehow, and I'm still not sure how, I survived and, later, thrived. But, when I look at how hard I had to struggle to achieve even a modest life and the deep suffering I endured for so many years of my life to receive a $13.69 per diem for five years of negative conditioning, familial alienation, and trauma is a complete insult. For so many Sixties Scoop kids, ten years in care is not unheard of. Their compensation, therefore, would amount to half of that. A mere $6.85 per day. And for the huge numbers of newborn babies apprehended and who spent eighteen years in foster care, the compensation is reduced further to $3.80 per day. And what of the adoptees? So many were placed in adoptive homes not only in communities distant from their own in Canada but in other countries as well, never knowing anything at all about their Indigeneity, about their proper place of belonging. While it's true that no amount of money could ameliorate the harm done, this is the way capitalist society determines value and importance. How ironic that compensation intended to set things right becomes just another statement of how little value is placed on the lives of Indigenous children.

Canadians, I believe, are beginning to understand that the residential school initiative was not some benevolent venture designed with the best interests of Indigenous people in mind. Rather, it was an implement in the colonial toolkit designed to destroy Indigenous identity. So was the Sixties Scoop and its continuing legacy in child welfare policy.

As the residential schools formally began closing down in 1969, the mandate for carrying on the mantle of destabilizing Indigenous families and communities was incrementally assumed by child welfare agencies in the various provincial jurisdictions. Unsurprisingly, given its history of a strong KKK presence, as well as having an influential member of the KKK as a member of Parliament for a number of years (Walter Davy Cowan), Saskatchewan was particularly zealous in its desire to remove Indigenous children from the influence of their parents and communities.

Although it is known as the Sixties Scoop, this drive to remove Indigenous children from their families actually commenced in the mid-to-late

1950s and persisted into the 1980s. Approximately twenty to thirty thousand children were apprehended. They were most commonly placed with middle-class, white families through adoption or fostering. There are exceptions to this timeline. For example, Buffy Sainte-Marie was scooped from the Piapot Reserve in Saskatchewan in 1941 and raised by a family in Massachusetts. This speaks to the fact that, while there are general timelines for the various policies relating to the apprehension of Indigenous children, what binds them all together is the relentless attack on Indigenous families and communities through the removal of children. From the opening of the first residential school in 1831 to the present day, this approach has changed somewhat in form but not so much in terms of intent.

Between 1967 and 1969, the Saskatchewan government established the Adopt Indian Métis pilot project designed to promote the adoption of Indigenous children by non-Indigenous families. This colonial offensive continued well into the 1980s. The province engaged in the wholesale apprehension of Indian and Métis children who were then placed in white homes either as adoptees or foster children. Upon apprehension, these babies were essentially advertised for sale. Newspaper ads featured photos and descriptions of Indigenous kids as though they were a patio set for sale or a puppy up for adoption.

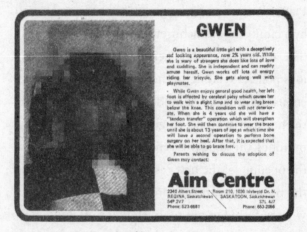

Apprehended Indigenous child advertised by the Saskatchewan provincial government through its Adopt Indian Métis program (Courtesy of the Provincial Archives of Saskatchewan)

Why would her sad countenance be described as deceptive? This is a child not quite three years old who was taken from her family. How could she be anything but sad, frightened, and in particular "wary of strangers." Likely the last strangers she encountered were the ones that took her away from her mother. Imagine the fear and confusion that child experienced and the impact that would have on the rest of her life. Imagine the thousands of children who suffered this fate and their families who were torn apart in this way.

Government of the Province of Sc. rchewan
DEPARTMENT MEMO

From G.E. Jacob, Director, Aim Centre   Date September 25, 1973

To   Mrs. D. Wilson, Supervisor, North Battleford   Your Ref.

Re   Award of Merit   Our File

      In recognition of your memo of September 21, 1973 pushing your region's permanent wards(who haven't been committed yet) you have been unanimously nominated by Aim Centre staff for the Salesperson of the Year Award which will be presented in due course and appropriate circumstances. In addition, your children, of course, will be entered for selection at the bottom of the list like all others subsequent to committal and we will wait to receive further news of children who may appear suspiciously adoptable.

                                   G. E. Jacob,
                                   Director,
                                   Aim Centre.

GEJ/mez
  c.c. Aim, Saskatoon

Correspondence from the director of the Adopt Indian Métis program proclaiming a social worker "salesperson of the year" (Courtesy of the Provincial Archives of Saskatchewan)

In fact, social workers were urged and rewarded for apprehending as many children as possible. An example of this is found in correspondence from

1973 naming a social worker "salesperson of the year" and encouraging her to identify "children who may appear suspiciously adoptable."

This begs the question, what does "suspiciously adoptable" mean? I remember in the '70s, there was a case in northeastern BC in which a social worker apprehended a child from a family living on their trapline. When asked to justify her decision to remove this child, the social worker stated that it was because there was no food in the house. In fact, the rafters were laden with row after row of dried game meat. Her reply to this? She thought the strips of dried game meat were rags. And herein lies the crux of the problem: the absolute power to make devastating decisions about the lives of Indigenous children was in the hands of white social workers who were entirely unqualified to assess wellness and sufficiency in an Indigenous context.

Between 1951 and 1979, a period of twenty-eight years, two out of three children were apprehended in Splatsin, a First Nation in BC. I believe this to be generally representative of the rates of child apprehensions in Canada at that time. In 1980, under the bylaw-making provisions in the *Indian Act*, Splatsin created and submitted a child welfare bylaw for approval by the minister of Indian affairs. It was rejected by the minister. The First Nation amended and resubmitted the bylaw and it came into force, not because the minister supported the shift of jurisdiction over Indigenous children, but rather because he failed to reject or approve it within the time limits set out in the *Indian Act*. The provincial child welfare authority initially refused to recognize the bylaw, sparking a massive, exceptionally well-orchestrated protest, the Child Caravan. The caravan started in Prince George and moved through a number of First Nations in the province, the number of supporters growing with each stop, and ultimately ended on the doorstep of the minister responsible for child welfare. She relented and an agreement was negotiated to devise a plan for the ultimate return home of the children.

Tellingly, this did not open the door for other First Nations to follow suit. The federal government closed the door on the possibility of any other First Nation asserting their jurisdiction over child welfare by creating a bylaw under the *Indian Act*. Splatsin remains the only First Nation in Canada, forty-two years later, whose jurisdiction over child welfare is acknowledged at law. Nonetheless, First Nations and Indigenous organizations, through decades of advocacy, litigation, persistence, and protest, have achieved a vastly larger role in child welfare policy development. Putting the federal and provincial governments' feet to the fire against their consistent resistance, we are saying there can be no more Tina Fontaines, no more Jordan River Andersons. At the tender age of five, Jordan, a Cree boy in Manitoba, died when the care he needed, approved when he was two years old, was never implemented due to a dispute between the federal and provincial governments as to which of them was financially responsible. Just as the residential schools were a life-and-death experience for Indigenous children, so too was the child welfare system, and often still is.

This wholly inadequate compensation under

the Sixties Scoop settlement only serves to remind us that we are seen as lacking in value as human beings. When we were placed in foster homes, we learned early on that we were not part of these families. We were commodities and, if these people were not compensated financially, we would not be there. This particularly stings when one thinks of the millions of dollars received by those managing these settlement agreements. Their work will be compensated so richly while, in comparison, the survivors' compensation is a pittance.

The devaluing of Indigenous life is not only evident in the Sixties Scoop settlement. The compensation package for residential school survivors was also deeply inequitable. Around the time Indigenous Residential School (IRS) cases were being settled through the Independent Assessment Process (IAP), a non-Indigenous woman commenced a lawsuit seeking damages for sexual abuse she had suffered at the hands of a Catholic priest at a private Catholic school. She suffered abuses similar to many IRS survivors. She won her case and was awarded damages in excess of $800,000.

The maximum compensation under the IAP was $275,000. A claimant could seek additional damages for loss of employment income, but it was rare for this to be awarded given the fact that so many survivors left the residential schools with virtually no education or skills and, as a result, had few employment opportunities and would not qualify for loss of employment income. Instead, they were eligible for compensation for loss of opportunity, but this was included in that $275,000 maximum compensation limit.

Someone had to come up with that compensation scheme. What was in their minds as they set these limits? I'm familiar with some of the arguments the Crown brought forward when survivors still had to proceed by way of litigation before the implementation of the Alternative Dispute Resolution (ADR) and IAP. At law, there is no time limitation for commencing a case arising from sexual assault. There is, however, an ultimate time limitation for bringing claims for physical abuse. It is well known that many children suffered unthinkable physical abuse at residential schools. Yet, the

Crown put forth the most despicable argument to prevent these children from being compensated. They submitted that because the children had been so harmed by the physical abuse, the court could not distinguish what harms arose from the physical abuse and what harms arose from other abuses. They argued that the children's lives had been ruined by the physical abuse and the court could, therefore, not distinguish between the harms caused by physical and sexual abuse. Since compensation for physical abuse was time barred, the Crown argued the survivor was eligible for no compensation at all. Over time, the Crown agreed to not rely on such technical defences, but both the ADR and the IAP compensation rules were structured in such a way to make it exceptionally difficult for anyone to succeed in a claim for physical abuse.

It is obvious that the compensation scheme arose from the same attitudes that were at the foundation of the IRS system. Indigenous lives were simply not as valuable as non-Indigenous lives. Even so, I don't dismiss the fact that many survivors benefited greatly from the opportunity to tell their story, to share the truth of their experiences. Likewise, some received compensation that was life changing and were able to use it in a positive way. On the other hand, for some, particularly those struggling intensely with the psychological impacts of the abuse they suffered, the compensation was life ending. Had the settlement structure been such that it supported community wellness, perhaps those people who didn't survive their settlement would have been able to receive the healing they needed.

Indigenous people suffered harm caused by the residential schools, not only on an individual basis but on a collective basis as well. Parents, grandparents, aunties, and uncles were deprived of their teaching relationships with children. The community at large was deprived of its roles in preparing their children to understand and take their place in the community. The tearing away of children from their parents, relatives, and communities left the social fabric of Indigenous communities in tatters. Yet, beyond time-limited funding for healing initiatives, the compensation schemes did not consider what was needed to help communities heal, strengthen, and re-establish their ability to provide healing and support to their members. The individualistic approach of litigation and alternative settlement processes did not address how to compensate communities for the harm caused by the residential schools. This is not surprising because it would have required Canada to support Indigenous communities in a return to self-determination and self-sufficiency. This, of course, is contrary to Canada's colonial agenda, which continues to seek a "final solution" to the country's "Indian Problem."

A frighteningly large percentage of the Indigenous child population ends up in care. According to the 2016 Census, 52.2 per cent of children in foster care fourteen and under are Indigenous, despite accounting for only 7.7 per cent of all Canadian children in this age group. This is not coincidental. It is well established that when the federal government decided to wind down its involvement in residential schools, the torch of Indigenous child deconstruction (the term used by Charles Henry Pratt, founder of the US Indian Boarding School system, and conveyed to his Canadian counterpart as the role of residential schools) and the further erosion of the Indigenous family and community was passed on to the child welfare system.

One need only consider the fourteen-year struggle to end discrimination against Indigenous children in care to see that destruction remains Canada's underlying political objective. In 2007, a complaint against the federal government was filed with the Canadian Human Rights Tribunal by the First Nations Child and Family Caring Society and the Assembly of First Nations. The claim alleged that child welfare services provided to First Nations children and families on reserve were discriminatory. Of course, filing with the Human Rights Tribunal was not an opening shot across the bow. It was more of a last resort in response to the predictable refusal of the federal government to respond to the evidence of discrimination without resorting to litigation. The Tribunal started hearing evidence in 2013 and the feds fought this case tooth and nail. A landmark decision was rendered by the Tribunal in 2016 in which it found that the federal government had indeed discriminated against, and caused harm to, Indigenous children in care.

That seems like it would be enough for the federal government to admit its failure to implement Indigenous child welfare equitably and to restructure its approach to Indigenous child welfare. That would be, of course, if we believed the government was driven by good intentions. But no. Instead, in the fall of 2019, after much foot dragging, the federal government filed for judicial review in the Federal Court of Canada. They petitioned the court to set aside the Tribunal's decision and dismiss the claim for compensation. In response to widespread criticism of this action, the federal government stated it did not dismiss the idea of compensation but believed that the Tribunal had operated outside of its jurisdiction in ordering compensation in a manner similar to a class action. I struggle to find a better example of weasel words. Why drag the matter out, causing increased cost and suffering to the complainants, if, in fact, it agreed with the idea of compensation? Well, it's because they did not really agree with the appropriateness of compensation. The case had dragged on for fourteen years and, despite the Tribunal's ruling, no one had been compensated. Now, bear in mind, at the same time that the federal government was arguing against Indigenous kids in court they were spouting platitudes about reconciliation. As Cindy Blackstock, executive director of the First Nations Child and Family Caring Society, once stated, "You cannot reconcile when you're fighting this generation of kids, the very descendants of the survivors from residential (schools)."

As the saying goes, talk is cheap. I am continually sickened by the disparity between the words uttered and the actions not taken by various politicians touting reconciliation. I am sure that a majority of Canadians hear the words of the federal government and believe they are genuinely making an effort to reconcile with Indigenous Nations. I am also sure they wonder why Indigenous people continue to critique government statements as inadequate. People's responses are similar to the horrible and ubiquitous question about the harms caused by residential schools: *Why can't they just get over it?* Canadians wonder, *Why isn't it enough?* It isn't enough because it isn't real. Reconciliation requires systemic change. It is not about rote land acknowledgements, apologies, and carefully staged public relations events designed to give the impression of a sincere effort. How can any of these things be taken as meaningful when we know what is going on behind the curtain? It is all high theatre.

Consider the recent papal visit and apology. Again, I recognize that some people were able to find peace in hearing the pontiff's words. But, for many, his words fell far short. Where was the acknowledgement of genocide against Indigenous Peoples through these schools? Yes, he spoke those words later, but not directly to the people who suffered it. Further, it cannot be ignored that the Catholic Church has failed to meet its financial obligation to survivors and its failure was officially sanctioned by the federal government and the courts.

The Catholic Church is one of the richest, if not *the* richest, corporations in the world. It is worth billions and billions of dollars. I remember visiting the Vatican Museum in Rome. The art and artifacts alone are worth billions of dollars without even considering the vast worldwide holdings of the Catholic Church. I will never forget seeing Nero's bathtub, a huge, circular stone edifice made of material that no longer exists on earth. The bathtub is described as "invaluable beyond calculation." So why not just sell off the tub and meet their obligations to survivors? It is beyond comprehension how the Catholic Church can express remorse while refusing to abide by the terms of a settlement they originally agreed to and still expect their words to be taken seriously. And what about those papal bulls, the ones that spawned the Doctrine of Discovery and its concept of *terra nullius*? These papal bulls provided justification for every violent colonial act visited upon us since first contact. Why then does the Catholic Church stubbornly refuse to repeal and renounce them? Catholic scholars claim it is not necessary to rescind these papal bulls as they have been abrogated and no longer underpin the approach or position of the

Church. Nonetheless, the spirit of the papal bulls is found in law, and it is necessary to rescind them to allow for change in the principles that underpin laws, including the laws that validate the claim that the Crown holds the title to Indigenous lands. When thinking of these contradictions, we also must remember that the Pope is not just the spiritual head of the Catholic Church. He is also the ex officio sovereign and head of state of the Vatican City State. He delegates executive authority to the president of the Pontifical Commission for Vatican City State, who is ex officio president of the Governorate and head of government of Vatican City. However, despite this delegation of authority, the Pope must also toe the political line, and he must stop short of undermining the foundation that nation-states rely on to disenfranchise Indigenous Peoples.

So, the pretty words, the pomp and ceremony, remain meaningless when the actions of church and state continue to undermine the healing, self-determination, and self-sufficiency of Indigenous Peoples in Canada and around the world.

These papal and government apologies must be more than performative; they must be more than carefully staged public relations stunts. Apologies must go hand in hand with substantive, systemic change, which, in turn, will support meaningful reconciliation.

In my mind, reconciliation in its most fundamental form is very simple. It's about restoring balance to the relationship between the Crown and Indigenous Nations. Think of the scales of justice. If one plate is laden with riches and the other empty, there can be no balance. Until there is a redistribution of the riches held by Canada and they are restored to Indigenous Nations, the scale will not balance. Monetary compensation is not sufficient, no matter how much it is. What is required for Indigenous Peoples to attain a return to self-determination and self-reliance are, at the very least, the following:

- a structural reorganization that will fully recognize Indigenous jurisdiction
- monetary compensation reflecting and reconciling historical economic inequity

- a return of lands with full recognition of Indigenous Title with an end to the notion of underlying Crown title
- a form of relationship similar to equalization that would see revenue taken from our territories, returned to our territories

No one wants to be rid of the stereotypical and mistaken notion that we are a drain on the country's resources more than us. We provided access to this country's resources, and the prosperity Canadians have achieved is wholly based on our agreements to share those resources with settlers. To achieve reconciliation, we must be beneficiaries of those resources in equal measure.

It seems so daunting, looking at what is needed to set things right. And it is. But I look at the tremendous successes Indigenous Peoples have achieved despite the brutality of the colonial experience. I look at what we, this tiny percentage of the population, have been able to accomplish despite the determination of the colonial agenda to wipe us out. If our people, deep in the immediate impact of residential schools and other forms of colonial violence, could nonetheless rise up and change the Constitution to forever re-entrench our rights in it, imagine what the non-Indigenous community could do if they used their privilege, stood up, and fought for us the way we did.

Recently, during a speaking engagement, I was asked if I was hopeful about the future. I replied that I was. The questioner wondered out loud, how, in the face of the devastation we have come through and continue to survive, I could remain hopeful. I replied, "How can I not be?" Just as that broken, abused child clung to hope for a better life against all odds, I now stand firm in hope and determination that one day justice will prevail. I am thankful, profoundly thankful, for a deep idealism I somehow never lost.

THE RISE AND RESISTANCE OF
INDIGENOUS LITERATURE

‖‖‖‖‖‖

Winston Churchill is often misquoted as saying "Gentlemen, history will be kind to me, for I intend to write it." Well, it's not exactly what he said, but paraphrasing his statement makes his meaning more apparent. What he actually said was "For my part, I consider that it will be found much better by all Parties to leave the past to history, especially as I propose to write that history." Regardless of the words, the meaning is clear. How we understand history is largely contingent on the perspective and objective of the hand that records it.

North American history has, by and large, been written by the colonizer and descendants of those who are not indigenous to this land. As such, history is more propaganda than a living record of the events and their impacts since European settlers first set foot on North American shores. The official story, the one taught to generations of Canadians, is not reflective of the flow of history as experienced by the first peoples of this land. To the contrary, Canadian history is written and told to create and support the idea of the supremacy and the myth of benevolence of the European newcomers.

I remember when the courts were first considering the admissibility of oral history in Indigenous cases, its reliability, and the weight it would be accorded. Simply stated, the court recognized that, for the most part, Indigenous history was passed down orally. This was not the only difference between the Indigenous and Western concepts of how history was to be recorded. Indigenous history was regularly dismissed as mythology because of the way historical information was conveyed from one generation to the next. While the Western tradition has employed a written approach to history, Indigenous history is conveyed through story and art. Indigenous oral history is a well-established social institution that ensured the transference of Indigenous Knowledge. Our stories are not told in the Western tradition. Rather, our stories are told within the cultural and social context of our peoples, from creation stories to the present. Given that our historical record is largely oral in nature, the style of storytelling often relies on symbols and other mnemonic tools. These are sophisticated records complete with characters who take on the role of telling the story. Scholars Renée Hulan and Renate Eigenbrod aptly describe oral history as "the means by which knowledge is reproduced, preserved and conveyed from generation to generation. Oral traditions form the foundation of Aboriginal societies, connecting speaker and listener in communal experience and uniting past and present in memory."[21] Our history is not contained in some dusty document in some government archive. It is three dimensional, a living history, as represented in our stories.

Unlike Churchill, we have not wielded power sufficient to control the narrative of Canadian history. However, with the burgeoning numbers of published Indigenous writers, the opportunity to tell our own stories is truly changing. The doors to the publication of Indigenous voices did not open easily, and prior to the 1960s, virtually not at all. The late '50s and early '60s were volatile times for Indigenous Peoples in ways that often seemed incongruous. Against the backdrop of the American civil rights movement, the burgeoning women's movement, and the rise of Quebec nationalism, among other things, Indigenous Peoples were contemporaneously thriving and struggling. For example, the brutal relocation of Inuit that resulted in the most horrific deaths by starvation was ongoing throughout the '50s and into the '60s. The Ahiarmiut from Ennadai Lake (now a part of Nunavut) were deemed by the federal government to be too dependent on trade with employees of a radio tower near Ennadai Lake. This small group of about fifty Inuit were airlifted to an island approximately one hundred kilometres away. Their tents were bulldozed, and they were removed, leaving behind all their possessions, including equipment for hunting and fishing. Members of the group died of starvation and exposure. The Ahiarmiut were relocated five times, with similarly deplorable outcomes. At the same time, in 1958, James Gladstone of the Blood Tribe was made Canada's first Indigenous senator by then Prime Minister John Diefenbaker. By 1962, Indigenous artists such as Norval Morrisseau and others were achieving national recognition. In the same time frame, in 1963, a Métis community was driven off its road allowance settlement near Yorkton, Saskatchewan, during the last of the Métis clearances. Through the '50s and '60s, the residential schools were still flourishing in the implementation of their hideous agenda. A deep defiance was brewing.

At the same time, Canada was working at creating and sustaining its own unique artistic and literary canon. In 1957, the Canada Council for the Arts was established to support and nurture the development of the arts and played a key role in what would be a burgeoning of representation of Canadian writers: the creation of a national Canadian literary canon. In the 1960s, we see the beginning of the literary careers of the likes of Alice Munro, Margaret Laurence, Leonard Cohen, Margaret Atwood, and others. But before them came *The Double Hook* by Sheila Watson, seen as a classic and a seminal book in the Canadian canon complete with its wooden and stereotypical characterization of the trickster. Of the early writers that included Indigenous characters or themes, only Laurence with her portrayal of the Métis Tonnerre family in her Manawaka series of novels (1964–1974) came close to a representation that went any distance at all beyond the stereotypes.

The '60s were hardscrabble years for the Indigenous Peoples of North America. Life was even more harrowing for Indigenous Peoples than it often is presently and without the reprieve of seeing Indigenous representation and success in virtually every walk of life, as we do now. We faced racism, hatred, violence, and a deep resistance to the raising of our voices, whether it be in the political or literary world. In the US, the

American Indian Movement engaged in some very high-profile direct-action events that served to heighten the awareness of the horrific treatment of Indigenous Peoples in North America.

On November 20, 1969, an occupation of the island of Alcatraz that occurred on November 9 of that year turned from largely symbolic in nature into an ongoing occupation of the island lasting until June 11, 1971. The occupation was covered by national and international media.

In 1972, activists engaged in a campaign supporting Native American rights known as the Trail of Broken Treaties. Caravans of Native North American activists travelled from the West Coast, and many points in between, to Washington, DC, demanding an end to federal government termination policies. The group occupied the federal Bureau of Indian Affairs and held it for a week, standing strong despite the negative press the occupation attracted. Their objectives were articulated in a twenty-point position paper that in effect structured Native American activism for many years following the occupation. They saw some success given that then President Lyndon B. Johnson revoked the US government's Termination Policy and promised it would be replaced by a policy in support of self-determination. In 1975, the United States Congress enacted the *Indian Self-Determination and Education Assistance Act*, Public Law 93-638.

And, of course, the occupation of Wounded Knee, South Dakota, was also a seminal moment in the emergence of Native North American activism. Approximately two hundred Oglala Lakota activists and AIM members occupied and took control of the town and its citizens on February 27, 1973. They demanded that the multitude of broken treaty promises be fulfilled by the American government. Police converged on Wounded Knee, within hours of the occupation, surrounding the town to prevent protesters from exiting and sympathizers from entering. What followed was an armed conflict and a seventy-one day siege.

Those years were also a time of powerful resistance in Canada. Let there be no mistake: Indigenous Peoples in Canada have been organizing their resistance to the ongoing oppression of modern-day colonialism as early as the late-nineteenth century. The organizations that sprung up in the '60s and '70s did not come from thin air; they followed on the efforts of early organizers. One such organizer, one of many, was Andy Paull, a force and a key figure in Indigenous resistance. Born in 1892, he attended St. Paul's Residential School. Starting as a teenager, he trained with a law firm for four years but never sought to be called to the bar as to do so at that time meant he would have been forced to give up his legal status as an Indian. Any Indian person who achieved a university degree was required to give up his or her distinct legal status. In 1927, as a member of the executive of the Allied Tribes of BC, he testified before a special joint committee in Ottawa on the matter of land claims in BC. In the same year, the federal government made it illegal to raise funds in support of efforts to resolve land claims. The Allied Tribes of BC disbanded shortly thereafter. Then, in 1945, Paul formed the North American Indian Brotherhood, which in turn dissolved in the early 1950s but provided a foundation for the ultimate establishment of the National Indian Brotherhood in 1968.

However, before that, in 1964, University of British Columbia (UBC) professor Harry B. Hawthorn was commissioned by the federal government to undertake a study and report on Indigenous life in Canada. The two-part report was published in 1966 under the title *A Survey of the Contemporary Indians of Canada: Economic, Political, Educational Needs and Policies*. For perhaps obvious reasons, the report has been since generally referred to as the Hawthorn Report and it served as a lightning rod for change. The Hawthorn Report found that Indigenous Peoples in Canada were disadvantaged and marginalized as a result of government policies and argued strongly in favour of self-determination under the heading of "Citizens Plus," a term meant to denote the retention of special status and the rights accorded thereunder, as well as the rights of all Canadians. The participation of Indigenous leaders and individuals in the consultation that informed the Hawthorn Report was predicated on their understanding that their involvement would lead to changes to the *Indian Act* consistent with the findings of the report.

In 1968, in response to the Hawthorn Report, the government of Pierre Elliott Trudeau began its own "consultations" with Indigenous leaders, and in 1969, Trudeau and his minister of Indian affairs, Jean Chrétien, issued the notorious *Statement of the Government of Canada on Indian Policy, 1969*, which would forever after be known as the White Paper or the White Paper Policy. The White Paper proposed an end to the distinct legal status of Indians in Canada. It also proposed vitiating all treaties entered into by Canada and Indigenous Peoples, dismantling the Department of Indian Affairs, and repealing the *Indian Act*. Reserve lands would be converted to private property. In summary, the White Paper was one of the most, if not the most, aggressive, open, and unapologetic initiatives of the Canadian government, which continued in its determination to implement a termination and assimilation agenda. Terminate the rights, assimilate the people. The White Paper embraced virtually everything contrary to every direction, suggestion, petition, or recommendation received from Indigenous Peoples during that faux consultation.

Around the time of the release of the Hawthorn Report, Indigenous Peoples came together once again to form a national organization and, partly, replace the earlier North American Indian Brotherhood. The National Indian Brotherhood was formed in 1968, with Walter Deiter from the Peepeekisis Cree Nation becoming its first president. In 1970, several Indigenous leaders[22] from across the country came together and incorporated the National Indian Brotherhood, with George Manuel taking over the presidency of the organization at that time. This was part of the unanimous and furious response of Indigenous leaders to the White Paper Policy. The expression of outrage at the content of the White Paper was like nothing seen before in Canada in terms of a unanimous response of Indigenous Peoples. Indigenous leaders grasped immediately that this was not a policy arising from the recommendations of the Hawthorn Report or the faux consultation engaged in the year before its issuance. The White Paper was instantly recognized as yet another attempt to terminate existing obligations that existed through treaty or other binding agreements and to erase any legal distinction between Indigenous Peoples and non-Indigenous people in Canada. The outrageously duplicitous efforts behind the White Paper actually served to coalesce Indigenous resistance.

British Columbia was unique from the rest of the country as a result of the fact that only a very few historical treaties were entered into, representing a small percentage of the land base of the province. The Union of BC Indian Chiefs (UBCIC) was established in November 1969 at a conference that saw over 140 BC First Nations in attendance. Chief George Manuel was the first president of the UBCIC. The organization formulated its response to the White Paper with a document known as the Brown Paper; its actual title was *A Declaration of Indian Rights: The BC Indian Position Paper.* The Brown Paper asserted continuing Aboriginal Title to lands in BC as well as a right to self-determination. It sought to protect the constitutionally entrenched relationship between Indigenous Peoples and the federal Crown and, thereby, the continuance of the nation-to-nation relationship that had existed there since contact.

The Indian Association of Alberta (IAA), under the leadership of Harold Cardinal, published its response to the White Paper under the title *Citizens Plus*, harkening back to the Hawthorn Report and its findings and recommendations. It was commonly known as the Red Paper. As the UBCIC staunchly defended the right to self-determination and Aboriginal rights and Title, the IAA was immovable in its support of treaty rights, the right to land, and the right to self-determination.

Other provincial-based Indigenous organizations also developed responses to the White Paper. Virtually all Indigenous organizations joined in protests and demonstrations expressing deep outrage and outright opposition to the termination agenda of the White Paper.

Today, no one would be surprised to see a delegation of Indigenous leaders on Parliament Hill in full traditional regalia. But, in the summer of 1970, this was unheard of. So, when on June 4, 1970, representatives of the IAA and the National Indian Brotherhood arrived in full regalia to a meeting with Trudeau and his full Cabinet, it had a stunning and unsettling effect. Following introductions, a prayer was sung by a member of the Blood Tribe in his language, with no translation offered. The policy paper was returned to then Minister Chrétien by Indigenous delegates, and Trudeau subsequently and bitterly shelved the White Paper and was quoted as saying, "We'll keep them in the ghetto as long as they want."

It was against this backdrop that Canadian Indigenous literature was trying to find a foothold. Before the '70s, there was very little on the shelves in terms of Canadian Indigenous literature. Likely the first published work by an Indigenous person in Canada, E. Pauline Johnson's *The White Wampum*, a poetry collection, was published in 1895. However, the '60s saw some movement when, in 1967, Chief Dan George delivered his "Lament for Confederation" to massive audiences, which played a role in sparking the imagination of would-be

Indigenous writers and a more optimistic sense of what could be accomplished in the publishing world. In Canada, in 1967, George Ryga published and produced his play *The Ecstasy of Rita Joe* at the Vancouver Playhouse to widespread acclaim. This play is credited as the first play in Canada to not only speak to the reality of Indigenous Peoples but to have Indigenous actors populate Indigenous roles on stage. The play was a touchstone. Even though it was written by a non-Indigenous person, it captured the essential nature of Indigenous heart, soul, and struggle. It attracted criticism from non-Indigenous corners in response to its unvarnished portrayal of the institutions of oppression in Canada and the damage they did, with intention to Indigenous Peoples. It also touched many non-Indigenous Canadians, in a positive way, causing them to reconsider their preconceived notions and beliefs about Indigenous people. And of course, Harold Cardinal's *The Unjust Society*, his nonfiction rebuttal to the White Paper Policy, was published in 1969.

Around the same time in the US, in 1968,

Kiowa author N. Scott Momaday published *House Made of Dawn*, which went on to win the Pulitzer Prize in 1969. *House Made of Dawn* is often considered to be the first literary work of what came to be known as the Native North American Renaissance. It was deeply instrumental in establishing publication as a meaningful possibility for aspiring Indigenous writers.

In Canada, by the early '70s, some Indigenous writers were finding a way through the resistance to the idea of Indigenous literary works. In 1973, Maria Campbell published *Halfbreed*, her powerful, unflinching memoir of the racism, brutality, and deep poverty experienced by Indigenous Peoples in Canada. Notably, without her consent or knowledge, her account of being raped by an RCMP officer was removed from her manuscript. She was not even made aware of this until she received her copy of the published book. That account has now been restored and included in a 2019 edition of *Halfbreed*. However, its original deletion speaks volumes to the challenges Indigenous writers faced in presenting our stories in a truly honest and reflective way. *Halfbreed* received critical acclaim at the time and became an instant classic that continues to educate and elucidate.

Maria Campbell went on to publish other important works, notably, children's books with a focus on traditional teachings. She wrote and produced plays, launched an academic career, and co-founded a film and video production company, Gabriel Productions, which was responsible for the creation of thirty-eight documentaries, among many, many other important accomplishments. At last count, Campbell was the recipient of twenty-two awards including honorary doctorates, the Order of Canada, Canada Council awards, and many others acknowledging her profoundly meritorious contribution to the creation of an Indigenous literary canon and in supporting and nurturing Indigenous arts. Critically, Campbell played a tremendously important role not only in inspiring Indigenous writers but also by mentoring them at her writers' camp at Gabriel's Crossing and through her endeavours in her illustrious career. Maria Campbell's work made a singular contribution to the foundation of Indigenous arts in Canada. At a time when this kind of work still faced significant resistance, her work in community theatre with Indigenous youth and her tireless advocacy for greater recognition for Indigenous writers went a long way in paving the road for a much wider acceptance of Indigenous literary works.

In 1974, the year following the release of *Half-breed*, Chief Dan George published *My Heart Soars*. After his powerful address in 1967, his "Lament for Confederation," his book found a receptive audience and slowly the doors started creaking open for other Indigenous writers. In 1975, Lee Maracle's first book, a memoir, *Bobbi Lee Indian Rebel,* was published. Between then and 2019 Maracle would publish seven works of fiction, four of non-fiction, three collections of poetry, and three collaborations. Of those seventeen contributions, only one was published in the '70s. Her next publication would not see the light of day until 1990. The only other Indigenous writers I can find who were published in the 1970s include Duke Redbird, *I Am a Canadian*, 1978 (poetry); Anthony Apakark Thrasher, *Thrasher . . . Skid Row Eskimo*, 1976, (memoir); Rita Joe, *Poems of Rita Joe*, 1978 (poetry); An Antane Kapesh, *Eukuan nin matshimanitu innu-ishkueu, I am a Damn Savage*, 1976 (memoir) and *Tanite nene etutamin nitassi? (What did you do with my country?)* 1979 (a novella); Minnie Aodla Freeman, *Life among the Qallunaat*, 1978 (memoir); and Basil Johnston, *Moose Meat & Wild Rice*, 1978 (short stories). Despite the illustrious literary careers some of these writers would later realize, the number of books published by Indigenous authors formed a tiny percentage of published works in Canada at that time.

But then, in 1980, Randy Fred, a member and now Elder of the Tseshaht First Nation, founded Theytus Books, Canada's first Indigenous publishing house, and operated it for forty years. Pemmican Books also came into being in 1980, the creation of the Manitoba Métis Federation, and was dedicated to the publication and promotion of Métis writers. The Gabriel Dumont Institute, also dedicated to Métis works, was established in 1980.

The En'owkin Centre, a unique and multi-faceted education facility dedicated to Indigenous education, was established in 1981 with Jeannette Armstrong taking over as executive director in 1986. As noted above, Indigenous-authored books were a real rarity leading up to the 1980s but, with the opening of three Indigenous-run publishing houses, things began to change. Pemmican Books published *In Search of April Raintree* by Beatrice Culleton in 1983 and, in 1985, Theytus Books published *Slash*, a novel by author and educator Jeannette Armstrong. Indigenous people were taking charge of the telling of our own stories.

The 1980s and '90s saw a movement among Indigenous creatives to establish venues, such as the En'owkin Centre, that would promote and encourage Indigenous authors. It was not until Indigenous creatives began establishing their own institutions to support publication of Indigenous writing that the notion of Native Literature began to take root. Following the establishment of the above-noted Indigenous publishing houses in 1980, Bunny Sicard, Denis Lacroix, and others established the Native Earth Performing Arts collective in 1982 (NEPA). Artist Shirley Cheechoo established the Debajehmujig Theatre Group on Manitoulin Island in 1984, a touring group that took plays into First Nations communities. The Committee to Re-establish the Trickster formed in 1986 with core members Tomson Highway, Daniel David Moses, and Lenore Keeshig-Tobias. In 1986, Tomson Highway became the executive director of NEPA. This was the first year NEPA had secure funding for a full year of programming and Highway produced his award-winning national hit play *The Rez Sisters*. The huge success of the play contributed further to a new age of Indigenous literary arts. In 1989, Armstrong, in collaboration with Lee Maracle and others, initiated the development of the En'owken International School of Writing. Around that time, Theytus Books began operating out of the En'owkin Centre. In 1990, Greg Young-ing, an established Indigenous writer and poet, took the helm of Theytus and dedicated himself to expanding the scope and access to publishing for Indigenous writers, collaborating with Randy

Fred, the Indigenous founder of Theytus Books, to promote Indigenous writers. By dedicating himself so wholeheartedly to the promotion of Indigenous literature and writers, in particular through his work with the Association of Canadian Publishers, Younging sacrificed his own career as a writer.

Jeannette Armstrong founded the literary journal *Gatherings: The En'owkin Journal of First North American Peoples* (1990–2003), which showcased the poetry and short prose of Indigenous writers. With the advocacy of poet Lenore Keeshig-Tobias, supported by the Writers' Union of Canada, changes were made at the Canada Council for the Arts so that Indigenous authors' grant applications were assessed by their peers. Keeshig-Tobias was part of the very active scene in Toronto in the late '80s/early '90s. She wrote the *Globe and Mail* article "Stop Stealing Native Stories" in 1990. She was then the founding chair of the Racial Minority Writers' Committee at the Writers' Union of Canada. In 1992, that committee organized "The Appropriate Voice" gathering, which led to the Writing Thru Race Conference. Held in 1994, this conference had a huge impact on Indigenous and racialized writing and publishing in Canada. Keeshig-Tobias was a poet, and, like others, her own writing was put on the back burner in favour of advocating for the establishment of an Indigenous literary canon. It took many years before her own books were published.

In 1993, Beyond Survival: The Waking Dreamer Ends the Silence was held at the Museum of Civilization (now the Museum of History) in Hull, Quebec. This international Indigenous arts conference was organized by a committee of Indigenous artists (including John Kim Bell, Jeannette Armstrong, and Al Hunter) and allies (including Victoria Freeman) and supported by the En'owkin School, and initially coordinated by Allen DeLeary and Kateri Akiwenzie-Damm. It was a hugely influential event that had ripple effects that are still being felt. Many collaborations and projects resulted, including the establishment of Kegedonce Press, another Indigenous publishing house. Kegedonce was founded in 1993 initially to publish the writing of members of WINO, the Writer's

Independent Native Organization, an Ottawa-based group of Indigenous writers and artists whose core members were Greg Younging, Joseph Dandurand, Armand Ruffo, Anne Acco, and Akiwenzie-Damm. Kegedonce then established itself as a dedicated Indigenous publishing house. Its motto is *w'daub awae*, Anishinaabemowin for "speaking true," and it remains an important member of the Indigenous presses of Canada today.

Daniel David Moses co-edited *An Anthology of Canadian Native Literature in English* (Oxford, 1992) with Terry Goldie, the first major Indigenous teaching anthology for literature courses, now in its fourth edition. The anthology showcased the works of many Indigenous writers published by smaller, less mainstream presses. It also introduced newer, younger writers, and Indigenous literature in Canada began to gain some momentum. The emergence of such collections and works established that not only did Indigenous literature exist, it was also a unique form more consistent with an Indigenous style of storytelling than with the strictures of the canon of English literature.

The revolution in making a place for Indigenous literature in Canada is not something separate from the Indigenous drive to resist the ongoing impacts of colonialism. Rather, Indigenous literature is an arm of that resistance. Writing and publishing our own literature makes a critical contribution to clearing the way for the restoration of our peoples to a place of wellness, sufficiency, and prosperity.

The work of these early trailblazers went a long way in demonstrating how Indigenous literature had its own form distinct from the Western literary canon and how the Western canon regurgitated a colonized perspective of Indigeneity. A perfect example of this would be W.P. Kinsella's *Dance Me Outside* and its portrayal of Indigenous people. His portrayal of a medicine woman as a drunk and his other characters as ignorant, unsophisticated buffoons with a propensity for violence reflected the diminishment and demonization of Indigeneity that was such an important aspect of the Canadian colonial agenda and, therefore, reflected in Canadian literature.

By the 1990s, the movement to establish a distinct Indigenous literary canon truly began to coalesce and gain momentum, the velocity of which has increased exponentially into the twenty-first century. As we have always done, we carved out a place for the expression of our art and the telling of our stories on our own terms within our own epistemology. The mainstream literary world began to take notice and now, in a little over thirty-five years, a minute historical span, Indigenous writers have left an indelible stamp, forever changing the literary landscape, with readers and publishers alike clamouring for more.

The Indigenous writers of today, myself included, owe an enormous debt of gratitude to those early trailblazers who broke down the walls to mainstream publishing by, among other things, creating our own publishing houses to promote Indigenous writers. The big houses began to take notice of these Indigenous writers and the rest is history. We went from almost complete exclusion to carving out space for our own voices in less than fifty years. A remarkable accomplishment.

And yet, there remain those, including readers, editors, and publishers, not yet cognizant of the fact that Indigenous literature is unique and reflective of Indigenous reality. For us, the Western literary tradition is an ill-fitting shoe. We simply cannot be forced to wear a shoe that will pinch our toes.

This creates a real challenge for Indigenous writers as not only do our traditional stories, filled with imagery, metaphor, and symbol, exist to convey ideas, they rarely, if ever, unfold linearly. They comingle ancient and modern times, and the nugget that sits at the heart of these traditional stories is an idea. An idea of how to live in the world in a good way. An idea of our place in the natural world. An idea of the proper ways to relate to each other. And many, many other ideas. These traditional stories reflect the epistemology of Indigenous Peoples from the beginning of our existence on earth. As a result, contemporary Indigenous writing very often follows a far more circular, dimension-defying style and structure arising from an idea that needs promulgating.

What is taken for granted in the Western literary canon and, therefore, doesn't need explication, is how it is contextualized by the Western version of history, culture, and social evolution. A non-Indigenous reader can take so many things for granted when reading from the Western canon. Those same assumptions don't apply to Indigenous writing and so, a kind of cognitive dissonance occurs when reading Indigenous works because they do not arise from the same context.

The negative and noble-savage stereotypes of Indigenous Peoples, created by design as part of colonization, in addition to the fact that Indigenous communities are very often distanced from towns and cities, create an "othering" of Indigenous people. In the eyes of so many, Indigenous people have failed to adapt to the modern world, and this is the reason for so much suffering in the Indigenous world. The opposite is the truth. From colonial times, Canada has refused to accept that we are not failing. We are seen virtually in every context as "survivors" of the various tremendous and terrible efforts to end us.

Gerald Vizenor, prolific Anishinaabe writer

and thinker, sought to find a word to better describe our place in the world. He posits that the term *survivor* is simply not enough to encompass all that we are, here and now. The term *survivor* conjures up images of someone living through a car crash or being stranded on a desert island, but somehow managing to live until rescued. In terms of using this to describe us as a people, it creates an image of a people hanging on by our fingernails, by the skin of our teeth. That is simply not us. In its place, Vizenor has repurposed an archaic word: *survivance*. Survivance is to survival what dominance is to dominant. It goes beyond the singular incident, the moment frozen in time, and reflects a state of being that encompasses everything we continue to be, following the moment of survival. Some describe survivance as the conjunction between resistance and survival demonstrating that Indigenous Peoples have not just simply survived. Rather, we continue to breathe life into our cultures in fluid, critical, and generative ways. Survival has a treading water sense to it, whereas survivance is reflective of the momentous and ongoing work being undertaken by Indigenous Peoples not only to resist the limitations inherent in the word *survival*, but in countering stereotypes imposed by colonial institutions through offering up authentic perspectives of ourselves, our culture, and our ways of being. This not only counters the stereotypes in literature such as Kinsella's drive to degrade, it asserts our own true knowledge, our epistemology, in our own style of storytelling.

The subtext in Indigenous literature is entirely different from that in the Western canon. Therefore, to truly appreciate, understand, and critique Indigenous writing, readers must locate themselves not in the context of Western civilization but in the historical, political, cultural, and social realities of Indigenous Peoples. For example, if a reader has never spent any casual time among Indigenous people, they will not understand the shorthand, the reliance on an Indigenous subtext in dialogue, and may judge it, negatively, according to a non-Indigenous conceptual framework.

What Indigenous literature is accomplishing, at a rate I wouldn't have dreamed possible when

I first began my life as an activist, is the placement of Indigenous reality on bookshelves right across the country. In every genre, Indigenous writers are at the vanguard of injecting our truth into the world, thereby modifying the Canadian fairy tale of its colonial history to reflect not only historical truth but how that truth remains deeply woven in the fabric of who we are today. Indigenous writers are doing what politicians can't. They are reaching into the hearts and minds of non-Indigenous Canadians. This is not to say that our stories, our truths, are accepted wholeheartedly by all. To the contrary. Deep racism and hatred still haunt us in both subtle and overt ways. However, this fast-growing Indigenous literary canon serves as an invitation and an inspiration to non-Indigenous Canadians to second-guess what they think they know and to take responsibility for their own education.

We created our own space in the literary world, just as we created the momentum to change the Canadian Constitution to specifically include that Aboriginal rights are Constitutional rights. None of this was just handed to us. All of this is part of our struggle to stand in the world as we are, not as non-Indigenous Canada would have us be. By insisting on the truth, Indigenous writers are contributing an invaluable service in clearing the way for substantive reconciliation; reconciliation that creates balance in the relationship between Indigenous and non-Indigenous Canada. That balance requires a return of land, resources, and recognition of Indigenous jurisdiction. With only 11 per cent of the Canadian landmass privately owned, there really is nothing stopping such restoration. Nothing, of course, except an abiding resistance, in the absence of truth, to move beyond the colonial imperatives that are firmly entrenched at the foundation and in the systems of Canadian society.

Indigenous writers play such an important role in fostering non-Indigenous understanding of who we are and where we stand; a necessary prerequisite to change. And we do it in our own way, pressing against the strictures of the Western storytelling formula, and any formula really, other than the telling-it-like-it-is formula. Strong and functional relationships are founded in truth and understanding. Indigenous writers do this critical work of telling the truth and deepening understanding in beautiful, creative expression without becoming either didactic or dull. There is a trickster-like beauty in that, and we are all standing on the shoulders of the Indigenous women and men who broke down the doors and made room for these necessary works.

CULTURAL PILLAGERS

||||||||

The Strange Phenomenon of Identity Fraud

T HOSE OF MY GENERATION GREW UP ON COW-
boy and Indian TV shows and movies that
perpetrated the idea of the ultimate superiority of
white settlers. The inculcation of such media, com-
bined with the false teachings of Canadian history
told in the classroom, was reinforced in the home
and the world generally and reflected in the play
of children. I remember it well. Children played
at being Indian, replete with pleather headbands,
multi-coloured feathers, and plastic tomahawks.
And, of course, everyone wanted to be the cowboys.
Who could blame them? The Indians always ended
up dead in pretend burnings, hangings, beatings,

shootings, and other inventive executions. However, the "Indians" were always stoic and noble, even when facing their dreadful demise. It was baffling to me back then. None of my Indigenous relations looked or behaved like that. Now I understand it differently. Just as children reflected the teachings they received in other childhood games, like playing house, or fireman, or soldiers, these kids developed their understanding of the relationship between Indigenous and non-Indigenous people based on the information they received at home and school. In particular, the ubiquitous myth of the inferior and dangerous yet noble savage. The hallmark of the Play Indian is an overblown, Hollywood-esque representation complete with all the visual trappings: costumes, tattoo identification art, face paint, feathers, and such.

These days, there are still settlers who just won't give up playing Indian. With the drive to indigenize the academy and for industry to have an Indigenous presence in their consultation processes, far too many of these imposters come to occupy places and positions that should be occupied by Indigenous Peoples. The arts are no exception. The problem is that these Pretendians are inserting themselves in places they have no right to be, promulgating yet another round of fabricated history and transferring the mantle of the noble savage to a new generation of Play Indians.

Pretending to be Indigenous is an act that transcends the individual. The phenomenon rises from a colonial imperative that works against us, just as all the other implements in the colonial toolkit work against us. Playing Indian and following the settler script of what "Indian" means is no different, and no less harmful, than any other colonial effort to apply a settler overlay on everything Indigenous, to create us in their own image and to expect our collaboration in their effort to do so. Just as church and state collaborated in their efforts to assimilate and terminate Indigenous Peoples, the Play Indian's construction of made-up ideas about Indigeneity works in concert with societal and governmental inaction regarding everything from the continuing quest for justice for our missing and murdered, to the wholesale apprehension and warehousing of Indigenous children, to the absence of potable water in dozens of Indigenous communities, and many other things on that long, long list of injustices.

False images of Indigeneity arise from people who are not Indigenous. True, they might run a DNA test and find that somewhere in the annals of history a soupçon of Indigenous blood is noted, but blood quantum is not how Canada (or Indigenous Peoples, for that matter) defines Indigeneity. Blood quantum is an American legal term and a complex, termination-oriented system used in the US to enumerate, and ultimately reduce, the number of Native Americans with recognized tribal affiliation. Rather, in Canada, to be legally recognized as an Indian, a person must meet a legislated definition. By the contortions of the relevant sections of the *Indian Act* (the *Act*), Indians are defined in Canada as those who meet the conditions set out therein. The word *Indian* is a legal term as defined by the *Act* and a word generically applied to the first peoples of what is now Canada. I specifically use the word *Indian* in this essay when I am referring to how we are identified in a legal context. It was used in common and unquestioned parlance through the colonial period and onward. In the search for more accurately representative words, Indigenous people began articulating preferences for how to be properly addressed. The nomenclature transitioned, starting around the early '60s or so and onward. We went from Indian to Native to Aboriginal and, most recently, to Indigenous when speaking of us as the first people generally. Increasingly, Indigenous people seek to be addressed by who they are, for example, Nehiyew, Anishinaabe, Nisga'a, Siksika, or Seneca.

Too many Indigenous people find themselves unable to meet the imposed standards that define the requirements of the *Act* to be a registered Indian. This is a direct result of the forces of colonialism and its concerted attempt to undermine the integrity of traditional Indigenous communities. Entire communities were relocated. Sometimes several diverse communities with different languages and traditions were lumped together for administrative convenience. Communities were, in effect, disintegrated by the forced removal of children and the criminalization of cultural, spiritual, economic, and governance traditions. For the longest time, provisions of the *Act* stripped Indigenous women of their legal status as Indians if they married non-Indigenous men. Their white counterparts, however, were accorded legal Indian Status if they married an Indigenous man. The children of those unions were recognized by the *Act* as Indian. Think of that. Matriarchs out, white women in. Further, joining the military, getting a university degree, and being called to the bar as a lawyer all at various times required a surrender of Indian Status.

Our people, victimized by the multi-headed spear of identity deconstruction, can be and often are denied legal recognition as Indian and, as a result, both membership and the right to participate in matters of importance in their communities. I was one of those people.

My mother, Martha Soonias, was the child of Charles Soonias and Sarah Wuttunee Soonias. Charles Soonias was the son of Chimichees (Jean), who was a direct relation of Mistahimuskwa (Big Bear). My kokum Sarah was the grandchild of Old Wuttunee, brother to Okimaw (Head Man) Red Pheasant and signatory to Treaty 6. The proper name for our place of belonging is not Red Pheasant, the name of the reserve. It is Mikisiw-wacîhk, the Eagle Hills. This is what my moshom, my grandfather, told me. He was born a mere seven years after the 1885 so-called Frog Lake Massacre.

In 1950, my mom married my dad. His father was English, his mother was French. In accordance with the *Act*, my mother's name was struck from the membership rolls of the Red Pheasant Indian Band, as it was known then. When she passed, I remember seeing correspondence from Indian Affairs in her papers confirming that her removal from the list was complete and attaching a cheque of about a hundred and twenty bucks to provide her the balance of her entitlements under treaty. Her identity as an Indian woman was erased. Stripping her of her Indian Status did not render her white. Only on paper. When my siblings and I were born, our Indigeneity was in our bones but not in our paperwork. We were not Indian according to the *Act* but rather characterized under the interesting term "non-status Indian." We were not Indian but not white, reminiscent of the "coloured" status in South Africa during the apartheid era. Though we maintained connections with our family at Red Pheasant, neither my mother nor her children had any legal rights to be there. We were born and raised 1,800 kilometres away from our homeland.

My siblings and I were fortunate in that we knew our family and community, even if we were so far away. We were never an integral part of the community beyond our extended family because of the distance, and though we visited and spent most of our summers there as children, that is not the same as being there day to day for birth, death, and everything in between. It wasn't until Bill C-31 was passed in 1985, in response to legal challenges about the discriminatory provisions of the *Act,* that we were able to reassert our legal rights as Indians. Bill C-31 provided a formula that restored Indian Status to some women and their children, but the criteria also excluded many people. There were several subsequent bills, each with a new formula for restoration of status, but each of these was also sown with discriminatory and exclusionary terms. The power remained with the federal government to define Indian Status, and so long as the federal government remains the arbiter of who is and who is not an Indian, Indigenous people will continue to be excluded. These "legitimacy" issues create deep complexities in terms of their relationship with their communities of origin, their place of belonging.

So, if Indigenous people who know their own genealogy going back multiple generations can be denied legal recognition of their Indigeneity by the convolutions of federal law, shouldn't these Pretendians be held to a commensurate standard when they claim to be Indigenous? Shouldn't they also be required to produce a painstakingly accurate family history to warrant calling themselves Indigenous? Something beyond a tiny spike on a DNA test? The double standard is beyond ironic.

Some people, including some Indigenous people, do not agree. They instead argue that requiring people who claim they are Indigenous to demonstrate the veracity of their claim is no different from the divide-and-conquer tactics used against Indigenous Peoples for hundreds of years; that outing Pretendians is a demand for proof of blood quantum, even though, as mentioned previously, the blood quantum test has never been used in Canada. I have yet to see a case in Canada in which Indigenous people demand that an imposter produce proof of blood quantum. Further, I agree with the critics of the blood quantum approach; first, because as a formula, it has no relevance or force of law in Canada. Second, because I believe there is much more to Indigeneity than biology. However, biology is a necessary indicator. I mean, really, would anyone claim to be Japanese or Italian or Ethiopian if they had not a single drop of Japanese or Italian or Ethiopian blood? Case in point, Hilaria Baldwin was outed for not being Spanish as she claimed to be. No one agreed with her stance that spending time in Spain when she was growing up made her Spanish. That is because it is a ludicrous claim. Claiming that a lifetime in the Indigenous community makes one Indigenous is equally ludicrous and, in fact, contrary to the very meaning of the word *Indigenous*.

In my novel, *Five Little Indians*, one of the characters gently counsels another, helping her see herself as being exactly in her place of belonging. He tells her she must not think of herself as a weed in the way non-Indigenous people would judge her; rather, she is a beautiful Indigenous flower. I extend the use of that analogy here.

Scientifically speaking, *native* plants are species that existed historically in an area. The Audubon Society's Plants for Birds program deliberately states that native plants are those that have "existed in a location prior to European colonization of North America."[23] These are the plant equivalents to Indigenous Peoples, the first peoples, the peoples here before European colonization.

Naturalized plants are so defined as those that spread into non-native environments and are able to reproduce in their new home and eventually establish a new population there. The land, the environment, essentially adopts them and gives them space to thrive. These are the plant equivalents to the non-Indigenous people who have a long history of association with Indigenous Peoples and communities in a good way and are welcomed and adopted into the community. They are legitimized by the community as belonging, if not Indigenous.

Invasive plants are non-native to particular ecosystems and their introduction is likely to cause "economic or environmental harm, or harm to human health"[24] (according to the National Invasive Species Information Center). These are the plant equivalents of identity frauds. They insert themselves, highly opportunistic in nature, uninvited, unwelcomed, and driven to overcome the native and naturalized plants, sapping all resources in that ecosystem for themselves, ultimately destroying that which naturally belongs there or has come to be accepted there. Just so, the identity frauds infiltrate and seek dominance, gobbling up resources, spaces, and positions of authority that rightly belong to Indigenous Peoples.

Despite the intentional splintering of our communities, we've carried on in ways we've always used, even prior to contact in terms of knowing each other and where we belong. We ask, *Who is your family? Where is your place of belonging?* True to our traditional methods of knowledge keeping, we did not need notarized documents or treaty cards to confirm citizenship. However, straightforward, time-proven methods such as these become more problematic when used in circumstances where the people seeking recognition are acting without honour or truth.

Some people argue that using the rules related to Indian Status is a colonial construct and inconsistent with the way Indigenous communities define themselves. While it is true that the definition of Indian Status found its roots in colonial legislation that was entrenched in the *Act*, one must remember that the first lists of who was to be recognized as an Indian were the lists of names of Indigenous people who identified themselves as such in the process of treaty-making. Those lists are reflective of our ancestral communities and their pre-Confederation understanding of who belonged in our communities. While the subsequent misuse of those lists through the contortions of the *Act* saw many Indigenous people denied membership in their own communities, it cannot be denied that those original lists were our own lists. As such, they augment oral history of who is related to whom and where they belong.

Others claim that the focus on outing Pretendians takes away from the important work Indigenous communities are undertaking to decolonize their ways of defining community and membership. While I agree that challenging Pretendians can be divisive, it's actually the Pretendians, the frauds, who create these divisions, not the ones attempting to protect Indigenous people from the destructive influence of the invasive species.

It is critical that we continue to call these people out for what they are. There are white supremacist groups and individuals whose false claims of Indigeneity are a new way of promoting assimilation and the extinguishment of rights that benefit Indigenous people only. One such example is Pat King, one of the leaders of the so-called Freedom Convoy, who declared himself to be Métis. Pat King was photographed holding a sacred pipe over his head like a flag, desecrating it, as he proclaims his Indigeneity despite saying that his purpose in life is to fight "against the depopulation of the white race." The white supremacist agenda is diametrically opposed to everything inherent to Indigenous rights. Why else would such people claim to be Indigenous except, in the way of an invasive species, to access, overwhelm, and destroy Indigenous people to ensure that it is the invasive species that spreads and prospers? It is reverse assimilation. They couldn't wipe us out with law and policy so they will try by flooding the rolls with fakes. For people who criticize those who stand against Pretendians, does that mean we should embrace the likes of Pat King, a known and unabashed white supremacist? I don't believe any Indigenous person would think that. At the same time, many Indigenous people acknowledge, honour, and embrace non-Indigenous members of our community that are fully *naturalized* into our community, accepting the roles, responsibilities, and limitations of their community membership.

That, of course, is entirely within the purview of the community to do. It does not, though, magically make that adopted member Indigenous.

The work of Darryl Leroux of St. Mary's University follows the emergence of the so-called Eastern Métis who have lost multiple court applications seeking to legitimize their status as Métis. His work further identifies and analyzes a long history of Pretendianism dating back to the 1600s. The term "aspirational descent" evolved from the academic works of Dr. Leroux and Dr. Kim TallBear, among others, and refers to Caucasians who claim Indigeneity even when it is roundly proven to be false. The work of Drs. Leroux and TallBear is critical reading for anyone interested in understanding the efforts of people like King to flood the Indigenous rolls with non-Indigenous people.

These identity frauds often seek to legitimize their claims to Indigeneity by expressing tenuous links, often to a single, solitary Indigenous person from hundreds of years ago, followed by hundreds of years with no connection to any Indigenous community. This kind of weak historical link does not create a right to identify as being of the Indigenous community. Think about it. Saying that such a tenuous link makes a person Indigenous is supporting a form of the blood quantum approach that is decried by those who disparage others for their work in outing Pretendians. For example, consider my circumstance as the child of an Indigenous mother and a French/English father. Let's say some genealogical history is undertaken, and it's discovered that there's a six-hundred-year-old paternal link to the British Royal Family. Can I call myself a royal? Am I entitled to be considered a member of the community the Royal Family comprises? Of course not. And why? Because being a member of a community is much more than finding a miniscule blood link from long ago.

In the world of the social scientist, the idea of what community means is measured by several factors. A community is a group of people whose connections and relations are formed by their shared history, traditions, experiences, geographies, and identities. Let's look at two high-profile cases: Joseph Boyden and the director Michelle Latimer,[25] both of whom doubled down on their right, if you can believe it, to Indigenous identity. Neither of them can establish any meaningful links, biological or otherwise substantive identifiers of belonging to any Indigenous community. Boyden claims his DNA indicates some Indigenous blood. However, regardless of the outcome of spitting in a test tube, those banking on DNA to demonstrate their Indigeneity simply cannot be considered Indigenous. There is no way of telling precisely when or how a drop of Indigenous blood ended up in a settler's DNA, and it certainly does not confirm membership in any particular group. How would such a person establish themselves as Indigenous pre-DNA testing? By way of what has always been done: identifying connections through shared history, community, tradition, geography, and family.

I often think of Mr. Boyden's insistent claim, articulated in the form of a meme: him proudly crossing his arms so we can see his feather tattoos and sporting a Chicago Blackhawks T-shirt completely tone deaf to the decades-long struggle to end the era of Indigenous people being reduced to sports team logos and mascots. He states, almost petulantly, "If I have been traditionally adopted by a number of people in Indigenous communities, if my DNA test shows I have Indigenous blood, if I have engaged my whole career in defending Indigenous rights, am I not in some way Indigenous?"[26]

No, Mr. Boyden, you absolutely are not. Even if he were adopted by an entire community, as opposed to a few individuals making space for him, that would not make him Indigenous. It would make him adopted, a naturalized plant at best. Just as an adopted child can never be made the biological child of the adoptive parents, a person adopted into an Indigenous community becomes welcomed and accepted as a member of the community but is not magically, suddenly Indigenous. Mr. Boyden claims to have defended Indigenous rights his whole career and that this advocacy should privilege him with the right to call himself Indigenous. Should every non-Indigenous lawyer who fought in solidarity with Indigenous Peoples for the recognition of our rights be considered Indigenous? Of course not. The very idea is preposterous.

For white settler descendants, domestic or settler hegemony goes hand in hand with a perceived birthright to everything. The residential school legacy and many other limitations and imperatives imposed on Indigenous Peoples were and are entrenched in the law. Virtually every aspect of Indigenous life has been legislated and controlled by policy arising from law. The history of this country is based on the taking of everything from Indigenous people. It is not controversial that Canada's colonial period (and postcolonial period) was and is nothing less than brutal for Indigenous people. Neither is it controversial that the deep harms done to Indigenous Peoples during colonial times remain and are often exacerbated by the systemic nature in which Canada continues to reflect its colonial foundation. And this is exactly where fake Indians find such a deeply ingrained sense of entitlement. They believe it is within their right, should they so deign, to usurp our very being and make it over in their own image. Interestingly, we did not see the extent of the plague of Pretendianism in the early days; the '60s and '70s. Why?

Because none of the Pretendian types would have wanted to be an Indian back then. It was just too damn hard, and there wasn't a pile of money in it: no rarified consulting positions, no fawning over the few Indigenous authors who fought their way into a place in the literary world, no well-paid positions in the academy that would ensure financial security and public idol-worship.

I began working with First Nations and Indigenous organizations in British Columbia in the '70s. As residential schools were closing and survivors were struggling with not feeling at home at home, there was a surge in the numbers of Indigenous people gravitating to urban centres. So, there were more people from Indigenous Nations located all over Canada working for First Nations and Indigenous organizations. Once I was working for a community that was of the Potlatch tradition. The community was planning a Potlatch in order for a young leader to receive his name. I was invited and welcomed to the Potlatch, but there was significant conversation among the Clan and House leaders as to where I should be seated in the Feast Hall. This is because seating at the Feast is organized according to Clan and House, and the hierarchy within each. This is an ancient governing structure that, for example, formalized leadership and responsibility for the management of territories and resources among other things. I did not belong to a Clan and, therefore, to no House either. So wherever could I be seated without offending the propriety of Potlatch? It was finally decided that I would be seated as a slave. Slaves in such communities experienced nothing like that of Black slaves in America. They were fed, cared for, and often lived out their entire lives in the community having families of their own. Their role was different from those who, in keeping with the analogy, were the native plants of that community: members whose membership in a Clan or House was delineated back to the beginning of time as the community knew it. Slaves were more like what I analogize as naturalized plants. They had no say in the business of the community, but they were treated well. I remember that Feast, and when the distribution of wealth occurred, as it does, I too, as a slave, received a very modest portion of that wealth, commensurate with my status in the community.

Likewise, in similar circumstances where I and others were working in communities we did not come from, our input was welcomed in the context of the work that we were doing there. However, when it came to fundamental issues that related to matters at the heart of the community, it was made quite clear to us that because we were not from there, we had no say in those kinds of conversations and no input in decisions about them. Limiting the say of outsiders, no matter that they were also Indigenous, these First Nations were protecting the integrity of their community. That is why it is important that the invasive plants are not given a voice in places they don't belong and in decisions they ultimately have no stake in.

Recently, there was the case of Carrie Bourassa, a professor at the University of Saskatchewan and the scientific director of the Indigenous Health branch of the Canadian Institutes of Health Research. During her tenure in both positions, she claimed to be Métis, Tlingit, and Anishinaabe when, in fact, she is Swiss, Hungarian, Polish, and Czechoslovakian. When evidence emerged that she was not Indigenous, she changed her story and claimed a right to Indigeneity by way of adoption by a long-dead Métis Elder. She held these important positions, positions that impacted policy decisions regarding Indigenous health for years until questions regarding the authenticity of her claims resulted in a third-party investigation. The report of that investigation, completed by Jean Teillet, has recently been made public. However, given that Bourassa resigned from the university prior to the completion of the report, it does not address her claims specifically. Rather, it focuses on the systems that allow and perpetuate identity fraud. In an interview with CBC, Teillet describes Pretendianism, saying, "It's poison. It seeps out everywhere and then everybody is tainted by it and everybody's damaged."[27]

It is horrific that for many years policy decisions impacting Indigenous people have been shaped by false notions of Indigeneity. Additionally, it is particularly egregious that, although she was raised by a white middle-class family, Bourassa repeatedly made claims of having suffered the impacts of colonialism that plague Indigenous people in the form of violence and family dysfunction. She made up tales of being engaged in traditional activities with her nonexistent Métis grandfather and claimed these helped her survive her allegedly difficult childhood. Her sister at one point also claimed to be Métis and, in Bourassa's own words, received large sums in the form of scholarships and education funds earmarked for Indigenous people. Presumably, Bourassa did as well in addition to claiming positions and roles that should be held by Indigenous people.

When questions were being raised about Bourassa, the university provost defended both Bourassa and USask's reliance on self-identification as a way of determining Indigeneity. Airini, the provost, unforgivably, went so far as to misquote the Honourable Murray Sinclair, suggesting he supported self-identification when in fact the opposite was true. The quote of Sinclair's statement that the provost used when read in full is the opposite of what she represented it to be. It was a statement that the honour system of self-identification is not working anymore and that new approaches must be considered and implemented. When this false declaration from the provost played out on social media, Sinclair's son responded with horror at this blatant misrepresentation of his father, shamelessly used to support USask's position on self-identification.

This institutional resistance to meaningful Indigenous participation is shocking particularly in the manner it treated the Indigenous faculty member who took it upon herself to raise the matter of Bourassa's false claims. As a result, this exceptional Indigenous faculty member left USask primarily because she just couldn't take it anymore, this unrelenting, systemic undermining of Indigeneity in the academy.

Indigenous critics of those who shine a light on identity fraud claim that doing so upholds colonial systems and undermines the efforts of Indigenous communities to develop their own definitions for membership. This is to argue that it is not possible to re-establish our own terms for membership while at the same time debunking false claims to Indigeneity. This is faulty reasoning. The development of Indigenous mechanisms for identifying those entitled to community membership is critical work. Identity must stop being something that is defined by law and policy founded in the colonial principles of assimilation, termination, and genocide. Accomplishing this is not hindered by speaking out against false claims to Indigeneity. The people who expose identity fraud, including the whistleblowers, are often subjected to abuse and harassment in their efforts to see Indigenous people in roles intended for Indigenous people or roles that are meant to serve Indigenous interests. This is something Indigenous people have fought so hard for and must not be minimized by faulty logic about the impact of outing Pretendians.

However, all of this is not to suggest that the issue is simple and without depth, nuance, and complexity. Many non-Indigenous people with no Indigenous ancestry whatsoever have married into Indigenous communities and have been welcomed, cherished, and valued. This demonstrates the ability of our people to determine who is a member of the community and who is not. This acceptance is yet another indicator of the beauty of our people. A person need not be Indigenous to become a member of an Indigenous community. It is the community though that must be able to decide this based on the facts. It is not something to be decided by self-serving imposters salivating at what they might gain from it. We do not want to be duped any longer. The sheer dishonesty of these fake Indians and their willingness to gobble up resources meant for Indigenous people and to take on prominent roles because they have misrepresented themselves as Indigenous is reason enough to expose them. It is, after all, a fraud.

Pretendianism is no different from the Indian agent telling the Indians just exactly how they are to be, stripping away the reality of being Indigenous. In addition to the beauty of who we are, our lives are characterized by the highest likelihood for poverty, violent death, suicide, incarceration, homelessness, and addiction. It's easier to embrace being Indigenous when you don't have to worry about being among the high percentage of women who are sexually assaulted or murdered; when you don't have to live on a reserve with no potable water; when you, or someone you know, is incarcerated because you can't afford a lawyer and stand no chance in a system riddled with systemic racism; or when your relative, like mine, might be dead because he was the wrong colour while looking for help on a country road. These terrible assaults on Indigenous people are among the shared experiences we have and which form our bonds of community and have done so for more than five hundred years. These fake Indians have neither the intergenerational knowledge that binds our people together as a community nor the intergenerational trauma, the scars of colonialism we uniquely bear, recognizable only to one another. As I wrote once in a poem, "we know our own relations by our star quilts made of ghosts." Interestingly, these Pretendians only pop up where lucrative opportunities await them. We don't see them volunteering to share the profound hardship so many of us live with. They do, however, feel comfortable claiming to have suffered as we have though they most certainly have not.

Take, for example, the outrageous case of Pretendian Mary Ellen Turpel-Lafond. Aside from having reaped the professional and, no doubt, financial benefits of faking Indigenous identity for decades, she claimed to have been born in and experienced a brutal and abusive childhood in the reserve community of Norway House. Turns out, she was born and raised in Niagara Falls and that both her grandparents and parents were Caucasian.[28] She countered the evidence collected by the CBC in its investigative article with the assertion that her father was Cree and had been adopted by her grandparents.[29] Her father's birth certificate, a publicly available document, was obtained and offers up the unequivocal truth that her father was not Cree. He was the natural-born child of her two Caucasian grandparents.[30] Like Boyden, Latimer, and Bourassa before her, Turpel-Lafond chose to double down on her false claims. This highly divisive, deeply disturbing case of identity fraud has spread deep ripples of dissension through the Indigenous community. This is one of the profound harms of Pretendianism. We have enough to deal with without having to find our way through such quagmires of deceit and disloyalty. Ironically, this situation pits Indigenous people against Indigenous people in defence of a non-Indigenous person. Admittedly, after over thirty years of fakery, it would be difficult for Turpel-Lafond to face down her lie and admit the truth. However, that is the only honourable option open to her. Perhaps it is too much to expect honour from someone who has based virtually their entire professional career on dishonour.

There is also the inauthentic and uninformed way Play Indians represent what it means to be Indigenous. In effect, they alter Indigenous reality by representing their fantasy notions and contrived ideas as real, wielding their privilege to render genuinely Indigenous people powerless to object or, importantly, to correct. So many Indigenous people who lost touch with their ancestry through colonial efforts at assimilation and termination suffer great loss and struggle through their lifetimes looking to reconnect with family, territory, and tradition. In the face of this, it is exponentially egregious when individuals already occupying a position of privilege use that privilege to assume an imagined persona as an Indigenous person. I went through this too.

When I was a young girl, maybe around nine or ten, I was very curious about the fact that my mother's skin colour was so much darker than my own. I always knew my mom was Cree; our summer visits to the reserve echoed with the soft sounds of the Cree language, an affirmation of that identity. I suppose I was trying to place myself in the world; to get a sense of what it meant to be Cree, French, and English. One day I wondered whether I would feel different if I looked different, if I looked more like my mom. What would it be like to look like what I felt like inside? Would the world make more sense if my ancestry was more visible? So, one day when my mom was out shopping, my dad was at work, and my siblings oblivious to me, I locked myself in the bathroom, found my mother's foundation makeup, and proceeded to apply it, generously, to my face and neck. I knew it had to be a rapid stealth operation given the seven-person household to one-bathroom ratio. I'm still not sure what I felt when I gazed upon this new version of myself. I blurred my vision a little and stepped out of myself as much as I could, to try and see myself as others would see me. Mostly, I felt that it didn't change me. In that moment, I knew that it was not the colour of my skin that made my mother, or me, Cree.

That was perhaps the first stirring of my curiosity about my place of belonging in this world. Growing up in a town far from our territory, I had an inherent sense that I did not belong. But I was also aware when we went to the Rez that I was family and, while our family was always welcomed with great excitement and happiness on those summer visits, I knew I was also from away. My sense of self would have been much clearer I am sure if I had grown up in my territory in Saskatchewan rather than far away in northern British Columbia. I spent decades learning our Nehiyew ways and finding my truth, all while being referred to as a pink Indian or a white lady due to my fair complexion. I was, at least, fortunate enough to know my community. Many do not.

The Pretendian phenomenon adds layers of complexity for Indigenous people trying to find their way home. As more and more fake Indians are exposed, some Indigenous individuals and communities are becoming wary of people who might very well be legitimately Indigenous. So many of our communities are generous and welcoming to people coming home. Yet, it is deeply embarrassing to be duped by frauds. Not wanting to be burned twice (or a hundred times), I see Indigenous people becoming more reticent about accepting self-identification. My beautiful, gentle Nokum would have welcomed any person into her home, made them tea, and fed them. Maybe she wouldn't have been so welcoming if she were being lied to in the way these fakes lie, slithering, insinuating themselves into places where they can take hold. This kind of fakery becomes a change agent in the Indigenous community, as open arms are replaced by increased suspicion.

After the outing of Michelle Latimer, Haida filmmaker Tamara Bell came forward promoting the idea of legislation similar to the American *Indian Arts and Crafts Act*. This act acknowledges the unique ownership of Indigenous art and levies hefty fines up to $250,000 and jail terms of up to five years as penalties for non-Indigenous artisans who fraudulently present their art as Indigenous. She notes correctly that Canada tends to turn a blind eye to this kind of fraudulent profiteering. I would add that Canada takes, at best, a *tsk tsk* approach. Or worse, literary and other luminaries defend fake Indians as though it is Indigenous people who are misguided in their efforts to protect our place in the literary, art, and academic worlds, places we did not enter easily or without struggle. Notably, the American legislation does not apply to literary works or film productions.

I believe that given these insidious, pervasive, and continuing actions by non-Indigenous writers and filmmakers, the time is right for comparable legislation in Canada. Such an act would be quite different in this country, given our legislative tradition of proportionality, and it would require the inclusion of literary and film works in its definition of art. Certainly, when a lucrative career can be forged on a false identity, and the fake Indians remain undaunted by moral outrage, there must be recourse in the law. Likewise, in academia, those who misrepresent themselves for gain should be prepared to face legal consequences. This is a fraudulent act. Fraud is actionable.

Every time another fake Indian is exposed, I feel as though someone has pulled the rug out from under me. I am incredulous that it's still happening. We can't go back in time and gently correct those kids with their plastic tomahawks. They are grandparents now. What have their children and grandchildren absorbed from those beliefs entrenched on the playground? Colonial attitudes of oppression are intergenerational. We are equally powerless to erase the discomfort and confusion of little Indigenous kids watching such games and how they add to the colonial browbeating that is a central feature in Indigenous lives. But, if we want to truly support the rights of Indigenous

Peoples, surely it must start with standing firm against fakery. No matter the quality of the work or art produced by these frauds, they must be held accountable for using their privilege to step over the backs of Indigenous people to reach for their golden ticket.

Expressions of the necessity for Land Back hopefully spark thought and further discourse (Courtesy of Janice Zawerbny)

LAND BACK

||||||||

No, We Don't Want Your Cottage

IN RECENT TIMES, THE LAND BACK MOVEMENT has gained a higher profile in reconciliation discourse. However, the Land Back movement is hardly new. In 1969, there was a critical moment in the conceptualization of Indigenous Title when the White Paper Policy sought to remove Indigenous rights from the Constitution, then known as the *British North America Act*, by attempting to end any legal distinction between Indigenous and non-Indigenous Canadians. In a despairingly familiar move, the federal government "consulted" with Indigenous Peoples concerning proposed legislative changes. However, the resulting White Paper sent a shock wave through Indian Country when it proposed the termination of the distinct status of Indigenous Peoples, which was in complete contradiction with the recommendations provided by Indigenous people in those so-called consultations. The White Paper stated that not only would the distinct status of Indigenous people be terminated, but all Indigenous lands would be reduced to fee-simple tenure, a move that ignored the collective nature of Indigenous land title and opened the door for the total loss of Indigenous-held lands.

Indigenous people gathered in the gallery at the House of Commons for the presentation of the much-anticipated White Paper, following lengthy discussions with government officials on the best way forward. Then Minister of Indian Affairs Jean Chrétien made the presentation, much to the horror of the Indigenous people present, many of whom had been involved in those consultations. Having participated in those talks in good faith, it was incomprehensible that the government would, in effect, produce a plan that was diametrically opposed to the aspirations expressed by Indigenous people. Completely ignoring the feedback of Indigenous people was no different from when Canadian civil servant Duncan Campbell Scott historically proclaimed that children dying like flies in residential schools was not enough for him to deter his course from complete assimilation of Indigenous Peoples into the Canadian body politic.

A great urgency was created among First Nations, and a Brown Paper out of BC and the Red Paper in Alberta were developed in response. The Indian Association of Alberta, under the leadership of Harold Cardinal, created the Red Paper, which was a comprehensive ninety-three-page response to the White Paper that clearly articulated what steps needed to be taken to respond to Indigenous oppression in a just manner. Largely adopted by Indigenous people throughout Canada, the Red Paper outlined, in great detail, a far different plan; one that would protect Indigenous interests, including recognition of rights to land, as opposed to the termination of them. The Red Paper changed the conversation on Indigenous autonomy by recasting it from an entirely Indigenous perspective consistent with the needs articulated by Indigenous people since first contact. Sadly, the principles of the White Paper, which advocated for termination and assimilation, remains the position of the Canadian government. While the White Paper was not accepted by Parliament, Jean Chrétien made it clear that the report would be shelved and presented again at another time. We have seen the essence of that White Paper in virtually every government initiative since. The government's intention to terminate us remains.

We have been having this same conversation for as long as I can remember. Indigenous people have asserted that the land is the very essence of our identity, our being, and that without it we will fade and disappear into the Canadian body politic, an achievement that was passionately and violently sought during the colonization of North America.

What we see in law and policy is deeply contradicted by what we see on the front lines. The Supreme Court of Canada recognized the collective nature of land title and held that when land title is established, the Indigenous people in question are free to develop that land, yet not in a manner that would be inconsistent with the collective best interests of the community both now and in the future. This same court held that the Wet'su-wet'en of British Columbia did not cede or surrender title to their traditional lands. Yet, in the face of profound dissent, Coastal GasLink is permitted, by the courts, to push a gas pipeline through these unceded territories. How is it that the arbiters of the rule of law can say they are determined to protect the collective interests of future generations and yet agree to let corporations destroy it?

Another example is the Mi'kmaq lobster fishery. The Mi'kmaq fishery has sustained that Indigenous community since before settlers arrived on their shores. Their right to fish and to sell their catch is articulated in the Peace and Friendship Treaties entered into with the British Crown in the eighteenth century. The terms of these treaties were the foundation of a peaceful relationship with the British newcomers.

In 1999, the Supreme Court of Canada upheld these treaty provisions and recognized these rights as protected under Section 35 of the *Constitution Act, 1982*. Nonetheless, conflict between Indigenous fishers and non-Indigenous fishers continues to erupt because Canada fails to incorporate the ruling of the highest court in the land into fishing regulations that will clearly articulate the nature of that right. This is not only a disservice to the Mi'kmaq, it is a disservice to non-Indigenous fishers who perhaps would be less inclined to resort to life-threatening violence if the regulations were made clear. It is hard to forget the incident in 2020 when approximately two hundred non-Indigenous fishers attacked Indigenous lobster pounds, damaging them, and set vehicles on fire. Indigenous workers were prevented from leaving the area and death threats were uttered. The RCMP responded by saying it wasn't a criminal matter. Is it any wonder Indigenous people are deeply distrustful of the RCMP? Once again, Canada failed to uphold the rule of law when it rules in favour of Indigenous people.

It is critically important that the rule of law is applied equally to Indigenous and non-Indigenous people. It seems ridiculous to even have to say that. However, in circumstances such as those faced by the Wet'suwet'en and the Mi'kmaq, and the countless similar instances throughout history, the colonizer has developed a strategy that allows them to ignore the rule of law.

First, they blame Indigenous people in cases where violence erupts. The Wet'suwet'en Hereditary Chiefs have been protecting their traditional territories peacefully. Never have they initiated violence. Yet, regardless that the rule of law rests in favour of the Wet'suwet'en, Canada responds with militarized police actions, violently removing and arresting the land protectors, giving the impression that it is the Wet'suwet'en that are violent and behaving in an unlawful manner. We have seen Elders and women violently arrested for protecting lands that Canada's highest court has found are theirs. Likewise, with the Mi'kmaq, in the face of extreme violence, the federal police force responds by refusing to protect the Mi'kmaq, claiming death threats and arson are not a police matter.

Another technique is to create confusion regarding the facts. Nowhere in the media coverage of the conflict with the Wet'suwet'en will you see government representatives explaining why it is authorizing the use of brute force to prevent the Wet'suwet'en from protecting their homelands, which are legally recognized as unceded.

Canada regularly minimizes the impact of the use of colonial force and domination by presenting a false notion of equality, that it is a confrontation between two equally situated sides. Of course, this is not the case. We are an oppressed people with none of the resources available to the Crown that would make us equal sides to a dispute. On the rare occasion when Indigenous people fight back, such as in the case of the Oka Crisis, Indigenous responses to violence are characterized as the source of the violence while the colonizers are portrayed as the victims.

This is the conundrum with every aspect of engagement between Indigenous people and the federal government. Out of one side of the mouth are promises of recognition, respect, and reconciliation, while their actions are simply a continuation of the colonial assimilation and termination agenda. How can we believe there is any modicum of honesty or good intention behind government initiatives when this impossibly contradictory dichotomy remains unresolved and uncorrected? Even in the language of the rule of law, we see this disparity. The Canadian rule of law is, ironically, a key implement in the colonial toolkit, used to oppress our people and silence our voices. Even when the highest court upholds Indigenous Title to our lands, it rejects our efforts to use our lands in our own interests.

However, through our tenacity and determination, Indigenous Peoples have progressed beyond the dark corners of our oppression. Our resistance has never been stronger, thanks to activism, advocacy, and the work of so many Indigenous people who dedicated their lives to creating and populating the national stage with Indigenous perspectives on just exactly what is needed for our return to a state of wellness and prosperity.

Another myth used to disenfranchise Indigenous people is the notion of Crown land. There is no such thing as Crown land. It is all Indigenous land. The courts have long held that the underlying title to the land rests with the Crown. Indigenous Title is a burden on Crown title, which acts like a lien. And how did this come to be? Through the Doctrine of Discovery. Relying on the notion of *terra nullius,* the colonial government and, ultimately, the Government of Canada simply declared the land as their own. *Crown land* is the term used to describe lands that the federal and provincial governments claim to own. Crown land is also considered public land. Authority for control of this "public" land rests with the Crown, hence the name. Less than 11 per cent of Canada's land is in private hands; 41 per cent is federal Crown land and 48 per cent is provincial Crown land.

Some will argue that First Nations who entered into treaty surrendered their lands in return for reserves and other forms of compensation that accrue through treaty provisions. The terms of some of those treaties even incorporate the term *surrender* explicitly. However, it has been legally well established that the spirit and intent of the treaties are to be upheld. In that context, we must ask: how would a people who did not conceptualize ownership of land as a possibility comprehend the term *surrender* as it pertains to the land? Indigenous epistemology has consistently defined the relationship between the people and the land as one of stewardship. The land was given to the people to sustain us, and in return, our obligation is to live in a manner that nurtures, sustains, and protects the earth. The truth of the matter is that Indigenous Peoples did not for a minute believe they were giving away their rights to use the land and its resources in return for tiny reserves and what would quickly become broken promises. The spirit of the treaties is that they were peace and friendship treaties. Indigenous Peoples were agreeing to share the land with settlers, not to disinherit themselves.

At the heart of successful and substantive reconciliation is the return of the land. Whether Indigenous Peoples opt to engage in Western-style economies or a more sustainable one in keeping with our obligations to the Creator and the land, we must have the land back. Without a land base, it is simply impossible for Indigenous people to return to a self-determining state. The end of economic dependence on the federal government is not only what Indigenous Peoples seek. The funding of First Nations has long been controversial among Canadians who believe it is their tax dollars that support First Nations, when, in fact, it is the wealth stripped from our territories that funds First Nations. Nonetheless, Indigenous self-determination would end the financial commitment to Indigenous Peoples beyond what is owed through treaty and other agreements. With 89 per cent of the Canadian land mass being public lands, it would be quite easy to begin the process of returning land to First Nations. This is the heart of the Land Back movement.

So, what exactly is stopping the Crown, with all its alleged support of First Nations, from returning the land? The idea of Crown land is rooted in eleventh-century Britain, where the law arbitrarily established that only the king could own land. Hence the term. The so-called New

World was considered *terra nullius* and the Indigenous Peoples populating the land to be ignorant, backward, and lawless. As the Doctrine of Discovery permits, the British were entitled to assert sovereignty over all the land contained in what is now Canada. This was imperial policy. It is trite that arbitrariness in law is anathema to democracy and the rule of law. So, how is it possible that, in the twenty-first century in a country that stakes its reputation on its dedication to democracy, such a critical notion of land ownership by the Crown is as arbitrary now as it was in the eleventh century, despite the fact that an entire legal tradition and infrastructure has been built around it to buttress the notion of its legitimacy.

In the early days of colonization, as the Europeans tried to take control of Indigenous lands, they quickly learned that Indigenous Peoples had a well-established system of laws and protocols. It didn't even occur to the colonizers that they might need consent, and they soon found themselves engaged in treaty-making with Indigenous Peoples based on the principles of Indigenous law. But making treaties did little or nothing to dampen the rapacious, imperialist appetite and the drive to control the entire land base. This is when the myth of Crown land took hold and, to this day, that archaic British law still is foundational to Canadian law, stating that Canada holds title to all lands not privately owned.

This myth colours the way the courts interpret treaties and even how to approach the question of ownership of lands (such as in most of British Columbia) where there are few treaties. The myth of Crown land also prevails in Canada despite the country's adoption of the United Nations Declaration on the Rights of Indigenous Peoples. The concept of Crown land effectively blocks the possibility of a return of lands to First Nations. A good example of this is the Tŝilhqot'in Nation title case, in which the Supreme Court of Canada found that the Tŝilhqot'in retained title. However, with the archaic law defining Crown land still on the books, the court found that the Crown maintained underlying title and could infringe on the land rights of the Tŝilhqot'in Nation if they could pass the infringement test established in the Constitution. Despite the fact the Tŝilhqot'in Nation was able to demonstrate the test for title, that is continuity of occupation, use, and unceded title, Canadian law is prevented from recognizing absolute jurisdiction.

Once again, colonial fingerprints are all over Canadian law and policy. The land can only be returned if the federal and provincial governments rescind the notion of underlying title to that land. Of course, they could do this with certain parcels of land, rather than the entire land base. Through good faith negotiation, the Crown could agree to rescind its self-proclaimed title to specific tracts of land to facilitate their return to First Nations. To do so would indicate the meaningful and clear intention to remove the thread of colonialism from the fabric of Canadian society. This is the choice Canada must make rather than simply waiting for our demise. It's been more than five hundred years; Canada should know we aren't going anywhere. Instead, we remain.

ACKNOWLEDGEMENTS

||||||||

ABOVE ALL, I ACKNOWLEDGE WITH DEEP GRATI-
tude all the Indigenous activists from the early
days; the ones who stood for us all, before the days
of well-funded organizations. My love to the determined literary Indigenous women who took
the lead and powered the movement to establish
an Indigenous literary canon, often at the expense
of their own literary careers. My thanks, heart and
soul, to Kateri Akiwenzie-Damm for her support
and assistance.

NOTES

||||||||

1. Truth and Reconciliation Commission of Canada, *Final Report of the Truth and Reconciliation Commission of Canada, Volume One: Summary: Honouring the Truth, Reconciling for the Future*, Summary of the Final Report of the Truth and Reconciliation Commission of Canada, (Toronto: Lorimer, 2015), 6.

2. "Glossary of Terms," Canadian Race Relations, 2015, https://www.crrf-fcrr.ca/en/resources/glossary-a-terms-en-gb-1/item/22808-colonialism.

3. James Daschuk, *Clearing the Plains* (Regina: University of Regina Press, 2014), 50.

4. Royal Proclamation of 1763 (October 7, 1763).

5. Daschuk, *Clearing the Plains*, 114.

6. Library and Archives Canada, Government of Canada Collections. Note to Big Bear from General Sir Fred Middleton, 1885, https://www.collectionscanada.gc.ca/canadian-west/052920/05292032e.html.

7. Truth and Reconciliation Commission, *Honouring the Truth*, 2.

8. Indigenous Corporate Training, "Indigenous Title and the Doctrine of Discovery," January 26, 2020, https://www.ictinc .ca/blog/indigenous-title-and-the-doctrine-of-discovery.

9. *"Terra nullius,"* Legal Information Institute, https://www .law.cornell.edu/wex/terra_nullius#:~:text=Terra%20nul-lius%20is%20a%20term,is%20not%20owned%20by%20 anyone.

10. *Constitution Act,* 1982, being Schedule B to the *Canada Act* 1982 (UK), 1982, c. 11.

11. Truth and Reconciliation Commission, *Honouring the Truth*, 12.

12. Universal Declaration of Human Rights, Article 1.

13. Daschuk, *Clearing the Plains*, cover notes.

14. Daschuk, *Clearing the Plains*, 153.

15. Daschuk, *Clearing the Plains*, 152–53.

16. Daschuk, *Clearing the Plains*, 50.

17. Daschuk, *Clearing the Plains*, 154.

18. Daschuk, *Clearing the Plains*, 154.

19. Mark Cronlund Anderson and Carmen L. Robertson, *Seeing Red: A History of Natives in Canadian Newspapers* (Winnipeg: University of Manitoba Press, 2011), 8.

20. Anderson and Robertson, *Seeing Red*, 19.

21. Renate Eigenbrod and Renée Hulan, eds., *Aboriginal Oral Traditions: Theory, Practice, Ethics* (Halifax: Fernwood Publishing, 2008), 7.

22. Noel Doucette, Andrew Delisle, Omer Peters, Jack Sark, Dave Courchene, Roy Sam, Harold Sappier, Dave Ahenakew, Harold Cardinal, and Roy Daniels.

23. Gabriella Sotelo, "What Is the Difference Between Native, Non-native, and Invasive Plants?" *Audubon*, February 25, 2022, https://www.audubon.org/news/what-difference -between-native-non-native-and-invasive-plants.

24. Sotelo, "What Is the Difference Between Native, Non-native and Invasive Plants?"

25. Barry Hertz, "'All I Can Do Is Speak My Truth': Filmmaker Michelle Latimer Breaks Her Silence after Indigenous Ancestry Controversy," *Globe and Mail*, May 11, 2021.

26. Joseph Boyden, "My Name Is Joseph Boyden," *MacLean's*, August 2, 2017, https://www.macleans.ca/news/canada/my-name-is-joseph-boyden/.

27. Jean Teillet as in Geoff Leo, "New University of Sask. Commissioned Report Tackles 'Poison of Indigenous Identify Fraud,'" CBC, November 3, 2022, https://www.cbc.ca/news/canada/saskatchewan/new-independent-university-report-tackles-indigenous-identity-1.6639470?__vfz=medium%3Dsharebar.

28. Geoff Leo, "Disputed History," CBC, October 12, 2022, https://www.cbc.ca/newsinteractives/features/mary-ellen-turpel-lafond-indigenous-cree-claims.

29. Geoff Leo, "Turpel-Lafond Now Claims Her Father Was Adopted from a Cree Family," CBC, October 14, 2022, https://www.cbc.ca/news/canada/saskatchewan/turpel-lafond-claims-father-adopted-from-cree-family-1.6617042.

30. Geoff Leo, "Birth Certificate Contradicts Mary Ellen Turpel-Lafond's Account of Her Father's Parentage and Ancestry," CBC, https://www.cbc.ca/news/canada/saskatchewan/birth-certificate-contradicts-turpel-lafond-account-father-parentage-1.6657129.

A NOTE ON THE BOOK ART

||||||||

THE ART THAT APPEARS ON THE FRONTISPIECE and jacket of this book is by Jim Oskineegish, a second generation Ojibwe woodland artist and member of Eabametoong First Nation. He currently resides in Sioux Lookout, Ontario. You can see more of Jim's work at https://jimi-oskineegish.pixels.com/.